# BODYGUARD
## TO THE PROPHET

Larry utilizing his survival training (see page 5).

Larry as the six foot perimeter man (see page 16).

# BODYGUARD
## TO THE PROPHET

### LARRY MULLINS

CFI
Springville, Utah

ISBN 13: 978-1-59955-336-8

Published by CFI, an imprint of Cedar Fort, Inc., 2373 W. 700 S., Springville, UT 84663
Distributed by Cedar Fort, Inc. www.cedarfort.com

LIBRARY OF CONGRESS CATALOGING-IN-PUBLICATION DATA

Mullins, Larry, 1936-
Bodyguard to the prophets / Larry Mullins.
    p. cm.
Summary: Personal experiences of the author from when he was one of the
bodyguards of Spencer W. Kimball, the President of the Church of Jesus
Christ of Latter-day Saints, with information about others supporting
Kimball, including his personal secretary, D. Arthur Haycock.
ISBN 978-1-59955-336-8
1.  Mullins, Larry, 1936- 2.  Kimball, Spencer W., 1895-1985. 3.  Haycock,
D. Arthur (David Arthur), 1916-1994. 4.  Bodyguards--Utah--Biography. 5.
Mormon Church--Presidents--Biography. 6.  Church of Jesus Christ of
Latter-day Saints--Presidents--Biography. 7.  Church of Jesus Christ of
Latter-day Saints--Employees--Biography. I. Title.

BX8695.K53M85 2010
289.3092--dc22
[B]

2009043220

Cover design by Tanya Quinlan
Cover design © 2010 by Lyle Mortimer
Edited and typeset by Megan Welton
Cover and interior photographs courtesy of the author.

Printed in the United States of America

10  9  8  7  6  5  4  3  2  1

Printed on acid-free paper

# Dedication

First, to my darling wife who encouraged me every step of the way.
When I lost my confidence in my ability to write something
that others would want to read, she would convince me
this was a story that needed telling.

To all of you who thanked me at the end of firesides about my experiences with President Kimball, and those who told me
you wished I would write a book.

To my friends, Michael Douglas and Chad Daybell.

Last, but not least, my family:
Kathy and Adam
Ann and Barry
Sue and Randy
Larry and Bonnie
Tracy and her family
Aaron and Melissa
Hannah and Steve
Aimee and our Indian family

And my thanks to all of our grandchildren.

# Contents

# Preface

A person might wonder why a book like this has taken so long—more than thirty years—to make it into print. It is a fair question, and one I need to address right in the beginning; otherwise, the question might cause the reader some confusion throughout the book.

Back in 1973, I was asked if I would be willing to serve as the bodyguard to the president of The Church of Jesus Christ of Latter-day Saints. One of the conditions was that I would not be allowed to tell anyone but my wife what I did for a living or what I would be doing at my job. At that point in time, the fact that security would even be needed for the President was thought to be too upsetting and nerve-stretching for the average member of the Church. A couple of months later, that restraint was relaxed a little—I was advised to tell my bishop and stake president; otherwise, they might think I had become inactive. So, for more than thirty years, I have been very low key about my experiences as the bodyguard for the President of the Church.

Then came the death of President Gordon B. Hinckley and the very widely televised funeral services, which most of us watched in fascination for hours. As I watched and listened to the various media people talk about what they were seeing throughout the morning, I became aware of the attention they were giving the bodyguard of President Hinckley. Time and time again they referred to him and his role in the prophet's life, not to mention the public role he was playing that very day. And as I continued to listen, I also heard various General Authorities make clear and unambiguous references to him as the prophet's bodyguard. For me, all of this was a little startling.

My first reaction was happiness. I felt happy that this wonderful man could be recognized for his many years of faithful service and devotion to the prophet he clearly loved and cared for. I confess, my eyes filled with tears as he entered the hearse alone and rode those last miles still watching over and guarding his beloved prophet. Even at the cemetery, he was shown keeping watch to the end.

My second response, however, was a little more selfish. I turned to my wife and said, "It's out!" As I sat musing, I began to realize that there was probably not a single member in the Church who did not know that the President of the Church had a bodyguard.

*Where does that leave me?* I wondered. It meant that I no longer needed to keep my experiences a secret. There are a great many things I have always wanted to say about my experience with President Kimball; things, in fact, I felt I *needed* to say. And there are a great many wonderful men who have served the presidents of the Church over the years that may appreciate someone speaking for them.

Just days after President Hinckley's funeral, an opportunity came to me to do a fireside about this very subject. I finally felt free to accept such an assignment. The fireside was well attended and well received, and it felt great being able to help members of the Church understand President Kimball in perhaps a different way than watching him in conference or on television. And then, only days later, I was asked if I would be willing to do this book. I prayed about it and received confirmation that the time was right and I agreed. While I recognize that I need to exercise wisdom in my account because it would be unwise to divulge any information that might compromise security procedures, I feel I can still tell my story. In so doing, I hope to help others understand why there is a need for security around the

President and share some personal insights about the man himself.

In John 17:3 we are told, "And this is life eternal, that they [you and I] might know Thee the only true God, and Jesus Christ, who thou hast sent." In one of the last and best sermons given by the Prophet Joseph Smith, known as "the King Follett Discourse," he focused on the same topic. It is not enough to know about God, we must come to really know Him. In the *Journal of Discourses*, President Heber C. Kimball remarked that Brigham Young's father, John Young, was the most like God of any man he had known while here in mortality. I was able to know one of God's prophets, Spencer W. Kimball, and he was the most like God of any man I have ever known. It is my desire to share with you what I know about him.

It has been said many times, "You got to know your limitations." I assure you, I *do* know mine. I am not a polished writer, but while I am not a master at crafting prose, I have a real story to tell. It isn't a story out of my imagination, but an experience I actually lived. Once in awhile, the real ought to trump the creative.

Some of my friends asked if I was writing my memoirs. I guess, in a way, I am, at least a couple of years' worth. There are several good books written about President Kimball. His son Edward wrote most of them. There is no way I could compete with that. But what I can do is tell you what it was like to be his bodyguard. It is my plan to keep my comments focused on what I personally experienced.

# 1

## The Bodyguard

"Last winter I got ready with my children to go
to the farm to kill hogs. Orrin P. Rockwell was going to drive."

—Joseph Smith[1]

**W**hy me?

I have asked myself this question more times than I can count.
I have come up with a couple of potential reasons.

The early 1970s were very perilous times for the President of The
Church of Jesus Christ of Latter-saints. Never since the days of the
Prophet Joseph Smith were the dangers surrounding the leader of the
Church as serious or life-threatening. Looking back, it is clear that
during the first two years of President Spencer W. Kimball's administration, the threats to the prophet's safety were serious beyond anything encountered in several decades.

As for my qualifications, I was big and very strong. I had already
received a great deal of training, which I will talk about later that prepared me to serve as a bodyguard, and I quickly developed a complete
and undeviating love and respect for President Kimball. While all of
this helped, it isn't why I was selected to protect the prophet at that
time. Perhaps the most important preparation came when I heeded the
prompting of the Holy Ghost to turn to the Secret Service. The training my team and I received in the Secret Service was essential for my
success as President Kimball's bodyguard. As far as I have been able to
determine, there has never been such a highly-trained team of Church
Security before or since; however, for most of those first two years, the
President's security was made up of men with Secret Service training.

Second, there was my own attitude about the position. This was not a job to me. It was an assignment from the Lord. President Kimball had my complete and total attention. The Lord knew I would be by the prophet's side every hour of the day and into the night. The prophet would never be left alone because of a casual attitude on my part. The Lord knew I would be a micromanager when it came to this assignment.

So, why not me?

I was born in 1936. Three days after I was born, my mother died from birthing complications. My father, overwhelmed with the responsibility for a new baby, decided to turn me over to the parents of my deceased mother. My grandparents were already well beyond the "child-raising" age, but raise me they did. They were the only mother and father I ever knew. According to my grandmother, Grandpa took to the responsibility of raising me, the child of his old age, with more enthusiasm than she had expected. I grew up quite literally walking in his shadow. He had been a successful rancher all of his life. He had a reputation as a great outdoorsman. He was a competent horseman, but in his old age he began to do a lot more walking. We hiked from camp to camp on foot. He seemed to come to enjoy doing it; it appeared to made him happy.

Those who knew him well might question that statement. One of his favorite sayings was, "The worst ride I ever had in my life beat the best walk all to pieces." Nevertheless, he did a lot of hiking, even when he didn't really have to. As we traveled, he would point out every plant he knew and what it was good for. We ate everything that could be eaten raw, and we cooked everything else for breakfast, lunch, and supper. He taught me how to build traps and snares, so we could add meat to our meals.

Grandpa was a renowned marksman with rifle and pistol. He worked with me until he was satisfied with my shooting ability. He taught me how to locate drinking water in dry, desert areas where others thought there was none. I believe he could have held his own against the best scouts and mountain men of any earlier era. He wanted me to learn those skills from him so they would not be lost. I tried hard and took pride in my skills as a backwoodsman. I did it to make him happy, and because I wanted to be good at it myself.

As I approached the draft age, I determined to enlist; it would cost me an extra year, but gave me more choices in picking how I would serve. I wanted to make sure I would be sent to where the action was. I was just a ranch kid from Utah and was a bit intimidated by moving out into the big world. When I began to rise to the top of my group during my first several weeks in basic training, it took me completely by surprise. It probably shouldn't have, because most of what I was being required to learn, my grandpa had already taught me.

Unfortunately, halfway through my basic training, I passed out while being force marched back to the barracks. I was put in a truck and dropped off at the barracks, where some of the men from my company dumped me on my bunk. Sometime later, I was still mostly unconscious, so they took me to the hospital. The medical staff told me later I should not have lived. My temperature was so high they didn't think they would it back down. I spent a couple of weeks in the hospital with what they called double pneumonia. Then I had to start my basic training all over again with a brand new bunch of guys. Soldiering seemed very easy for me, and I did it very well. I was made what we called a "shirt sleeve corporal"—a temporary rank that only applied to basic training. Everything I was allowed to shoot proved easy, and I qualified at what they called an expert level.

After successfully completing basic training, I moved onto advanced training. I received an assignment to a demolition training unit and began adding special skills to my list of things I would use as a bodyguard later. Not long after being assigned to a more permanent base, I was picked to train as part of an aggressor unit. My battalion was preparing to take part in a large stateside battle operation. My aggressor unit would be the guerrilla warfare contingent and would be acting as the enemy. This turned out to be the unit where the training was the most intense.

We had specialists from Fort Benning brought in to push us day and night. I learned more in those few short weeks than I had in sixteen weeks of basic training. Our training had a heavy emphasis on escape and evasion, with guerrilla raids designed to take high level prisoners. This also proved to be of great value in future bodyguard work. When that operation came to an end, I was relocated to a new base where the army began to train me for jungle warfare.

The major goal in my mind was to prepare for warfare in Korea, so jungle warfare didn't make a lot of sense at the time. In hindsight, it seems to me that the military may have been thinking about Vietnam a long time before there was any general idea that we might be involved there. At any rate, in the middle of all this, word came down that the army was going to test for the much coveted Expert Infantryman Badge (EIB). Each base would run their own tests—each starting with several hundred applicants until they pared that larger number down to the twenty or so that they would send to the main test.

That year, they had picked my base, Fort Polk, Louisiana, as the place where the main test would occur. That seemed to be the reason why Fort Polk worked hard to make sure their final twenty were the best they could prepare. Fort Polk started the selection process with five hundred applicants. I was surprised to learn that I had been selected in that number. As it turned out, I was selected because of my high scores. These were mostly physical fitness scores, rifle and small arms scores, hand-to-hand combat and bayonet scores, and other scores of like nature. At the end of the Fort Polk testing, I was even more surprised to learn I had scored high enough to be picked in the top twenty.

Then began the main test. Groups of twenty or less began arriving from bases all over the United States and even from bases overseas. Now I was up against serious competition. As I recall, the total number of those being tested was a few short of six hundred—about the same number as what we started out with at Fort Polk, but the number was comprised with the best from each base. I must admit, I was having so much fun being tested, I wasn't even thinking about ending up in the top twenty, but that's exactly what I did! And then, almost without realizing how it happened, I was up on the stand being awarded the much desired EIB. As designed, twenty soldiers were successful in earning this award. Of those twenty, sixteen were officers, one was a master sergeant, two were sergeants first class, and I was at that point in time, a private. For me, a promotion went along with the award. I got my first stripes.

So it was, as a private, first class, that I tried to push my new found influence and applied for an overseas assignment. I was pushing for Korea, but my papers came in for Germany. As I was boarding the boat to ship out, a group of us were pulled off and sent to Fort Dix for reassignment to Panama. After a short time spent in Fort Wm. D. Davis, near Colon, Panama, I was again reassigned to the army's Jungle Warfare Training Center (JWTC) where some serious preparation for my later role in life really began.

JWTC is not a regular army base. It is, as the name implies, a training center. Everyone assigned there is an instructor as a part of a training cadre assigned to teach the skills needed to fight in the jungles. My main assignment was to teach jungle survival skills and techniques. I also taught escape and evasion, sniper skills, demolitions, guerilla warfare tactics, and tactics focused on taking down high-level targets. In addition, the commander of the center, a crusty, old, battle-hardened colonel, picked me to be his personal security (more normally referred to as his adjutant, aide-de-camp, or other less complimentary terms that might be used by the men). Now, the position of adjutant is unique because it is always defined by the commander himself. Different commanders often see the adjutant position in totally different ways. To some, the adjutant is nothing but an errand boy—someone to bring his refreshments, carry messages, or even shine his shoes. My commander was too much of a historian for that. He recognized that the higher your rank, the higher value target you offered. He used and trained his adjutant as someone to cover his back and protect him from anyone who might bring him harm; and thus began my first real training as a bodyguard. I had gained some reputation on the rifle team, and was at that time one of the top shooters on the U.S.A.R. C.R.I.B. pistol team. I was also on the U.S.A.R. C.R.I.B. boxing team.

My commander had confidence in all the other qualifications I needed to be a bodyguard. He saw to it that I would have access to any other training I might need to improve my ability to protect him. By the time I left the U.S. Army, I felt I could provide as good a level of protection as any man in the business. Many years later, while being trained by the U.S. Secret Service, I could not help but marvel at how few new things they had to teach me.

Back in civilian life, I had a great many other jobs, but in the middle of all that, I spent several years with the Burns Detective Agency and with the Webb Detective Agency, working in the areas of security, investigation, and protection. In addition, I built something of a reputation for developing training manuals and organizing programs and policies for groups and organizations to work from. This will make more sense later as I move into my time with Church security.

After I moved back into civilian life, I did all the normal things. I married the wonderful light of my life, Patsy Selman. Together we had a large and wonderful family. From oldest to youngest: Kathy, Ann, Sue, Larry, Tracy, Aaron, Daniel, and Hannah. In addition, we had two wonderful Navajo foster children. Aimee, the oldest, we had through middle school, high school, and even into college. Jerry, her brother, we only had a couple of years.

During this time, I ran survival programs, served as the president of two different corporations, and as program director at several colleges. I ended up as the director of the outdoor survival programs at Brigham Young University. Although there are no survival programs at BYU presently, back in the sixties, the program at BYU was the premiere program in the nation. Other colleges and private programs came to us for answers and guidance. When I left BYU to join Church security, the plan was always to return as soon as I was finished. But, as usually is the case, if you stay away too long, there won't be a place for you when you are ready to return. I'm reminded of the wise old German who said, "We get too soon old, and too late smart." I have no regrets—my life has been a wonderful ride—bumps and all.

Because this book is going to be about the next period in my life, I see no need to put anymore here in this chapter. But I will add that I spent a little over a year in Church security working mostly on training manuals and on training security personnel until the day I was called into the security director's office. I was told they were planning to organize a new section intended to provide protection for the president of the Church and asked whether I could put together the training needed for the men who would be working in that section. Well, that's what I was already doing with security in general, so it seemed a natural question. I said I could. Then they asked me if I would do that training. Going back to BYU was beginning to look further off in the future. I answered that I would be happy to do that. Well, it seems there's always an "oh, by the way," which came this time in the question: "Would you be willing to serve as the commander of that section once its up and running?"

I think it was then that I realized I might never teach at BYU again. I remember hearing myself agree to accept that responsibility. Two years or so later, I walked back into my old department at BYU. I sat down and had a great little visit with the man who had replaced me. He had been my right hand man when I was the director, and he was a very good friend. If it had been on my mind to move back into my old position, I pushed the thought out of my head that day and moved on to another life. I still feel good about that decision to this day. It would have been cruel and unfair to him; besides, I would have missed the great ride I have had since that day.

At times, the assignment was extremely rough, but I wouldn't have traded it for the world. I have had a wonderful time serving people. There are a number of people alive today that wouldn't be if

I had not been there to rescue them. I spent around twenty-five years in an area of law enforcement where almost every night I went to bed knowing I had done some real good in the world that day. That is a feeling to which no price can be assessed.

I have to say I have loved my life. I don't want to suggest that its always been wonderful. There has been much pain and much sorrow, but in the end, the good and great things have outweighed the hard things many times over. Always there has been this wonderful woman at my side. When I did pretty well, she was there to tell me she was proud of me, and when I really screwed up, she was the one to support and encourage me. My children have always made me proud, my grandchildren are now making me proud, and my great-grandchildren are growing up and adding to my warm and happy feelings. Life is wonderful, but truth be known, I can hardly wait to step through the veil and find out if there is anything President Kimball needs me to do for him.

1. Lyndon Cook and Andrew F. Ehat, *The Words of Joseph Smith* (Provo, UT: Grandin Book Co., 1991) 374.

# 2

## The Assignment

"I am positive in my mind that the Lord has planned our destiny."
—Spencer W. Kimball[1]

As I said before, I often asked the question, "Why me?" And a number of people over the years have asked, "Why you?" What did I have going for me that would cause a number of administrators to see me as the best person to fill this position; to look at that in that kind of isolation would leave out the most important power in the process—the influence of our Heavenly Father. I have never doubted that my Father in Heaven carefully engineered me to be ready, at that precise moment in time, to accept the responsibility to begin the process that would make the protection of his prophet a smooth and organized transition. In that capacity, I always knew I would be serving as a usable tool in his almighty hand.

Now before I move on, I need to talk about my response. Over the years, people have asked me how I could respond to such a request, seemingly without trepidation. Well, I want to assure you my feelings at that time were bordering on pure fear. Yet, at the same time, I had an assurance that I was right where I was supposed to be, responding precisely as my Heavenly Father would have me respond. I was almost overwhelmed with a sense that everything in my life up to that point had been to prepare me for just this challenge. That night, I could not sleep as I replayed the many events in my past that had clearly been preparation for this assignment. I am now in my seventies; looking back over the years, I can say that never in my life was a sense of importance so clearly evident as it was in that one special moment. Everything in my past had prepared me for and led me to that one question.

Perhaps there are those who wonder how could one be so arrogant as to think they were worthy and qualified to assume responsibility for the life of God's prophet. I remember a comment made to me once by a Church leader. He said "I believe both you and your team are a waste of money. You are not needed. Surely God can protect his own prophet." Clearly, God can and does protect his own prophet. However, I'm sure we all remember President Kimball's counsel: "God watches over us, but it is usually through another person that he meets our needs." That person is acting as a tool in God's hand to accomplish the thing we are praying for. So, again, God does protect his prophet, but sometimes that protection comes through men on earth who he has prepared and qualified for that particular task. No right thinking man would dare think of himself as the protector of God's prophet without God standing behind him, providing that man with the guidance and power to make the task possible. To think anything else would be foolishness at its utmost.

I accepted the assignment because I had total faith that God had prepared me to succeed and that he would be there with me every step of the way to make me equal to the task.

One thing I have gained a strong testimony of over the years, especially during the years I spent with students out on the survival trail, was the reality of Satan. I know he is real, and that we are all fighting a daily battle with him and his minions. Some people foolishly think that his influence would be the lightest around the prophet, but ask yourself this question: who would he most like to destroy? Destroying God's prophet would be the most serious damage he could inflict. God knows his own enemy better than any of us. He knows he must guard his prophet every minute of every day. Those of us who try to help with that endeavor know we must be ever vigilant, but God is always in charge and always in control. We are, at best, simply tools in his mighty hand.

Still, it is not enough just to want to help. Many probably wanted to help President Kimball with his heart problems, but only those with years of careful preparation, such as Dr. Russell M. Nelson, could realistically be of much use. So it is with security; every Church leader, every General Authority, indeed, every member of the Church would love to step in to try to protect the prophet; but without the skills, ability, and training to do the job, they would not only be unable to help, but they also would actually get in the way and would most likely make the problem worse.

These were the kinds of things that were on my mind, as I assumed the responsibility of this assignment. Satan would be bringing his most serious efforts to bear on destroying President Kimball and on defeating our best efforts to protect him. I was told I would be working under the supervision of a wonderful man—a former law enforcement officer from Canada—by the name of Murray Ford. Together, we set out to put a plan in place, which eventually became known as the new Personnel Security Section to cover the President of the Church, who, at the time, was President Harold B. Lee. President Lee was a big man. I was 6'4" and about 250 pounds, so it was suggested I should be able to blend right in. As you will see later, that turned out to be something of a joke.

One of the first things Brother Ford and I had to deal with was what kind of men we should be looking for. At the time, to be a good security guard meant that one must be member in good standing, worthy to hold a temple recommend, honest, trustworthy, in reasonably good health, and willing and able to work whatever schedule they were asked to cover.

This new assignment would require a lot more from these men. We had to be sure that if a situation suddenly deteriorated, we could count on these people to come through without any mistakes. To insure this kind of quality, we would need to develop methods to test for the qualities we felt the job would require. We tried to set up a number of ways to see how quickly a man could make decisions. A person who tended to take a long time to decide little things, even insignificant things like a choice between several good soda pops or candy bars might have a problem making bigger decisions quickly. If a man was riding along with the prophet and something dangerous suddenly erupted in his face, could he react quickly or would that small mental lag get the President hurt or worse? Well, we simply didn't feel we needed to take those kinds of risks. We had to do our best to eliminate those kinds things before putting someone on the team.

To make matters even more complicated, not only did the individual need to be a decisive person, but he also had to be extremely flexible. If the decision he had made didn't seem to be working out, he needed to be able to adjust his plan on the move, so to speak.

Another thing we needed to test for was an individual's ability to be extremely observant. We set up training rooms into which we placed applicants for a set period of time. After removing the applicant from the environment, we had them describe to us what they had observed while in the room. While we understood that someone can be trained to become a better observer, we wanted to start with those who showed a greater inherent ability at the beginning.

We tested for the ability to stay focused and for physical strength. We interviewed applicants to determine if they were able to state a willingness to put the prophet's life ahead of their own. We listened for their stated belief in the whisperings of the Holy Ghost.

Over time, we began to thin out the ranks until we had a list of men we felt we could trust. In the end, we had a list of twenty-four men—all seasoned security guards—that we were told we could train. The full-time team, of course, would be much smaller, but this would give us a good list we could pull from in any special event or situation.

When training began, it became my responsibility to organize the training materials. While I had faith in my ability to put together a good training manual, it didn't make a lot of sense to try to reinvent a wheel that was already working and in place. The United States Secret Service was already training a great many good men to serve as bodyguards to the President of the United States of America. They were the experts in this field—the only people who did the kind of thing we were preparing to do. There are a lot of people who think they are able to do this kind of work. But just because you have been a police officer, or a FBI Special Agent does not qualify you as a bodyguard.

It didn't make sense to look to any other agency. The Secret Service was the only show in town who trained its people to do the kinds of things we were trying to train our people to do. I reasoned that they just might be willing to share some ideas with us, or maybe, if we were really lucky, some training materials and manuals. After all, what would it hurt to ask? I made an appointment with the Western Regional Director, Tony Sherman, and sat down to state our request. His response was most surprising. "We are very concerned" he said, "about your President and the level of his coverage. We will be very happy to help you in any way we can."

As it turned out, the vast majority of the training done for our people was done by Director Sherman and a number of his agents. This has no precedence that I am aware of. For the first time in the history of the Church, the men who would be providing bodyguard security for the President of the Church were trained by the Secret Service of the United States of America. That training took place over a several weeks and was done at a level agreeable to Director Sherman. I do not believe this has level of training has ever been repeated since that time. That team of men was arguably the most qualified and prepared group of bodyguards the Church has ever produced.

When a man accepts the responsibility for the life, health, and well-being of the prophet of God, he ought to feel he has been as well trained as is humanly possible. Yes, we always count on the Holy Ghost, but we should not expect the Holy Ghost to have to work in a vacuum. When a man has been fully trained mentally and physically, it gives the Holy Ghost something to draw on. Although it would be possible, we do not expect the Holy Ghost to make a brain surgeon out of an individual who hasn't even gone to medical school. If it seems to you that I am overworking this point, it is because no one single issue has been harder to get administrators to try to understand. I was always asked why we needed all of this training. Why couldn't we just rely on the Spirit? Surely it would tell us what to do. Ironically, the prophet himself never took that position. He believed the more training we had, the more effective we would be.

It might surprise you to hear, as the prophet's bodyguard, I found I had to learn to take orders from a great many bosses. A bodyguard works for the prophet, but he also answers to the prophet's personal secretary, the guard's own security supervisor, the director of the security of the department, and the director of the personnel department, and that is only a listing of those in the official line of command. But then, if any of you reading this have ever worked at any kind of job, a flow of command like what I have just described isn't likely an unknown concept to you.

Well, while getting fully trained is important, we always found ourselves being pushed by some kind of deadline. In this case, while we were trying to become highly trained, the prophet was in need of protection. President Lee had a bodyguard during this time, but he was only one man, and he was completely untrained for the assignment. Hurry, hurry, hurry was the watchword. Get things together, get organized, and get him a well-trained protection team. Just when we felt we were finely ready, the worst thing imaginable occurred. President Harold Bingham Lee died, and I was devastated.

I had been looking forward to getting to know him. I had spent a great many hours dreaming about just how wonderful that was going to be. And, in a short moment, all the hard work and service we were ready to provide him was moot. We spent our only real service to him standing over his casket while thousands of heartbroken members passed by to wish him a fond good-bye.

1. Spencer W. Kimball and Edward L. Kimball, *Teachings of Spencer W. Kimball* (Salt Lake City: Bookcraft, 1995) 37.

# 3

---

# A New President

Each one of you has it within the realm of his possibility to develop a
kingdom over which you will preside as its king and God."

SPENCER W. KIMBALL[1]

Spencer Woolley Kimball was nearly seventy-nine and had been
an apostle for thirty years at the time of his call to the Presidency. His health had been so bad that President Lee had said of
him, "Spencer is being kept alive from one blessing to the next."
Even though he stood next in line, he never thought he would have
to worry about becoming the prophet. President Lee was younger
and much healthier, and almost everyone felt he would be around
for a long, long time. I do not believe there was anyone in the
Church as devastated by the death of President Lee as was Spencer
W. Kimball. Not only did he love President Lee more than most of
the Brethren, he now had to step into a responsibility he had hoped
to avoid.

I personally testify to one and all that Spencer W. Kimball
hoped he would never need to assume that role of prophet; he truly
did not covet the position. But here it was staring him in the face.
The one thing anyone who knew him would know was that he
would shoulder any burden that his Heavenly Father called upon
him to shoulder. So, on December 31, 1973, Spencer W. Kimball
sat down before the media with President Nathan Eldon Tanner, his
first counselor, and President Marion George Romney, his second
counselor, to officially begin presiding over not only The Church of
Jesus Christ of Latter-Day Saints but also the world.

As the commander of the "Personal Security Section," which, in reality, meant the bodyguard team of the president of The Church of Jesus Christ of Latter-Day Saints, I was responsible for selecting and training the members of the team. I was responsible for the level of coverage and everything involved in the operations of the activities of the President's coverage. My individual responsibility was what is known in the Secret Service as the "six-foot perimeter man." I was responsible for the six feet directly around the prophet. If you were to draw a six-foot circle around the President, I would be responsible for everything that happened within that circle. This meant that in order to control any danger that might be occurring inside that circle, I would have to be inside that circle at all times.

Let me try to make this a little more clear by using an ancient metaphor. Let's say we have a king (representing the prophet) inside a castle. Now, to protect that king, there would be a number of defenses in place. First, the castle might be built on high ground, which forces the enemy to charge uphill, slowing them down and exhausting them at the same time. Next, there would be a large area cleared of trees and vegetation, making the enemy more vulnerable to the king's archers. Then there would likely be a moat followed by an outer wall the enemy would have to breach. Inside the main wall there would be at least one more additional wall, and finally the castle keep. If the keep is ever breached, the only thing left to protect the king was his "shield wall," or wall made of the king's best knights. These men stood in a circle around the king, locking their shields together, and giving up the king only after they were all dead.

In many ways, the protection for the President of the Church was like this, and the six-foot perimeter man was like the king's shield wall. The six-foot man had a special responsibility as the final wall, as it were. So, while we operated as a team, I was generally referred to as "the bodyguard." I was the one closest to him, the one most visible, the one others needed to be the most aware of. And if that were not enough, I was also the section commander. Still, we were all bodyguards. And so it was on the first working day of the new year (1974) that a new prophet and a new bodyguard met.

I knew he had been briefed concerning this new program and fully understood what his personal security was all about. What remained was for him to meet me, the one he would have to deal with the most.

I remember the long walk from the security director's office to President Kimball's new office. I was filled with fear and trepidation, not just in meeting the prophet, but a real fear that he might not approve of me and that he might ask to have me replaced by someone else. I had not forgotten that one of the things the supervisors liked about me was my size and that I could blend in well around President Lee. Well, President Lee was more than a foot taller than was President Kimball, and I was taller than President Lee.

Brother Hallingshead, the director of security, and I entered 47 East South Temple at the rear underground door and proceeded down the hall to the elevator. As we stepped off the elevator onto the main floor, we were met by D. Arthur Haycock, the personal secretary to the prophet. I immediately noted how the security director deferred to him. Another wave of fear ran through me as I suddenly realized that here was someone else who could reject me with the wave of his hand. D. Arthur ushered us into the President's office. President Kimball had already left his desk and had come around to be at a place where he could greet us almost before we were in the room. Brother Hallingshead began to introduce me, and President Kimball had already extended his hand to me. I took his hand and looked into his eyes. I can still remember today having something of an out-of-body experience. I was there and taking part in a real world experience, and yet, at the same time, slightly aware of another place or dimension. Nevertheless, the thing that impressed me the most at that moment was a message delivered into my mind: "This is God's chosen prophet." It was not spoken in words, but rather it came to me as a concept, fully formed, more powerful than words could have ever been. I remember thinking that I already had a testimony that he was God's prophet and this impression was meant to strengthen that testimony. But as the impression came several more times while I served him, I now believe there was something more involved, and I'm not at all sure I can say I fully understand it to this day. Clearly, for some special reason, it was important for the Holy Ghost to clarify, cement, and bind me to my new responsibility.

The meeting went well, and I felt immediately attached to President Kimball. I thought of myself as a low-level servant and yet he, the prophet of God, treated me with the same respect he showed to other General Authorities or major Church administrators. I always think of him whenever I read about the experience that Joseph and Oliver had with John the Baptist on the banks of the Susquehanna. The Savior himself said of John: "Among those that are born of women there is not a greater prophet than John the Baptist" (Luke 7:38). And yet, when Joseph and Oliver tried to worship him, he told them he was just a fellow servant. I think President Kimball had the same attitude. He saw all who held the priesthood and strove to serve the Master as fellow servants. I was immediately filled with great love for this man, which love only continued to grow over the period of time that I served him.

I believe we all go through life somewhat chained to the image we have of ourselves. I believe that President Kimball saw himself as a leader for God's purposes and that perhaps he saw himself as an emerging prophet. Early in my life, I found I had the propensity and aptitude for the skills needed to be a highly proficient warrior. Because that is the self-image that I seemed to be chained to, I naturally gravitated to something I could do to serve my Lord and Master using the gifts I had been given. For me to end up as the bodyguard to God's prophet was not much of a surprise to many who knew me well. So, here we were, both of us at the point in life we had been prepared for, both overwhelmed by the awesome responsibility, but both aware that we had been prepared for that responsibility. He got to leave this mortal experience while still in full harness. I was not so lucky. President Kimball was close to perfection. I had a great deal yet to make straight. So, here I am, more than thirty years later, still trying to get to a point where I can follow him. Maybe finishing this book will help.

During our first day together, we tried to get as many of the other members of the team introduced to him. It turned out to be only two, as I recall. Clearly, it was important that he be able to recognize all those on his own security team. However, President Kimball had a full schedule of activities that day, and we couldn't take too much time on security matters. So, when Director Hallingshead left, I was left in the care of D. Arthur Haycock (hereafter referred to as simply "D. Arthur"). We sat down and began to reorganize things around this new concept of close security. I quickly learned that everything ran through D. Arthur. He was often referred to by various General Authorities as the "Majordomo," the director, the manager, the master butler, the maitre d'hotel, the guardian, the proctor, and a great many more titles we don't have time to list.

D. Arthur had been the personal secretary to four Presidents of the Church: George Albert Smith, Joseph Fielding Smith, Harold B. Lee, and Spencer W. Kimball. He was obsessively protective of "his" (as he liked to call him) president. He took me on as an extension of that protectiveness, and I immediately saw him as my real boss in the sense of who would be giving the orders, and before the first day was over, we had become a team. I learned to love and respect D. Arthur as I have few others in my life. We had the same mission, caring for the prophet, and we were always on the same page with regard to how that should be accomplished. I have never worked for anyone in my life that I enjoyed working for as much as D. Arthur Haycock. He ordered a desk to be brought down and placed just outside the door to his office. That was to be my workstation while President Kimball was in his office. Anyone coming to see President Kimball had to first pass by my desk, then pass through D. Arthur's office. D. Arthur would then announce the visitor before he was allowed to enter President Kimball's office. This arrangement was, I'm sure, at times uncomfortable to the President, but it was completely necessary to secure his safety. Whenever he left his office, I was right there at his side. There was never any need to look around to find the security guy, because I didn't wander. If he was in his office, I was at my desk.

1. Kimball, *Teachings of Spencer W. Kimball*, 31.

# 4

## The Threat

*"I remember what Joseph said a short time before he was slain . . . He said:
"Men are here today who are seeking my blood, and they are those who
have held the Priesthood and have received their washings and anointings;
men who have received their endowments."*

—Wilford Woodruff[1]

While Joseph Smith was yet a young lad, well before he had his remarkable "First Vision," someone tried to shoot him from a hiding place. The bullet missed him and struck a cow instead. It was almost as if Satan discovered him at that point in time; it seemed that from that time on, his life would be always in danger. It appeared that Satan knew who he was and wanted to remove him before he could do any of the things he had been foreordained to accomplish. While Joseph was still a young man, one of his neighbors, a young man a couple of years younger than him, assigned himself the task of protecting Joseph. His name was Orrin Porter Rockwell. For the rest of their lives, that was precisely the role he played. He was the first bodyguard in this dispensation.

Today there are those who wonder why the president of the Church needs a bodyguard. Well, as you can plainly see, the position goes back to the beginning of the history of the Church. During the Palmyra period, Joseph's life was in constant peril. It was then that Porter Rockwell began to learn his craft. He became, perhaps, the best pistol and rifle shot to ever carry a gun. But then, he was also likely the only one who received help from above. Mobs and assassins stalked Joseph from place to place. However, these enemies were from the outside.

When we get to the Kirtland period, a more devastating kind of enemy began to endanger the prophet. This new enemy was coming from within the membership of the Church. At this time, the threat on the prophet's life became so great that he had no choice but to flee. The Prophet Joseph's mother, Lucy Mack Smith, recorded, "The persecution finally became so violent that Joseph regarded it as unsafe to remain any longer in Kirtland, and began to make arrangements to move." One of the last things he said to the Brethren was: "One thing brethren is certain, I shall see you again. . . . I have a promise of life five years, and they cannot kill me until that time is expired."[2]

This statement shows he was taking the threats very seriously, and he clearly accepted the fact that he could be killed but not before the time the Lord intended. Church historians today generally agree that the core of the enemy at that time was made up of apostate former members. Sadly, we all know that Joseph was eventually martyred. For the sake of understanding the need for Church security, especially as it relates to the president and prophet of the Church, it is important that we all understand just who the enemy is, and back then, who the enemy was. At a meeting of the city council in December 1843, Joseph states: "I am exposed to far greater danger from traitors among ourselves than from enemies without."[3]

However, President Cannon really gets to the core of the problem in this quote:

> Do you doubt the existence of a devil and or evil spirits? Have you not seen his spirit manifested? You have seen men and women in this church who once were faithful and devoted to the work of God; but they fell into sin, and another spirit took possession of them. Men as high as members of the first Presidency have done this. I remember very well William Law, counselor to the prophet Joseph, a friend of the prophet, a friend of God apparently, a staunch man in the church; but he committed sin, and that man, who had occupied that high and exalted station, compassed the death of that prophet. He was one of the chief conspirators in arranging plans for his destruction, and took an active part in urging on his martyrdom. Members of the council

of the Twelve also partook of the same spirit. It is the secret that Satan possesses; for Jesus said of him that he was a liar and a murder from the beginning. He is seeking constantly to destroy the work of God, filling men with his spirit, and urging them forward to acts of deadly hate, even to kill and to destroy. That is the spirit of Satan, and we see it manifested in men.[4]

We should also never forget that Judas was one of the Twelve Apostles.

In my instructions to the security team for President Kimball, I reminded them about these historical facts. I told them to trust no one fully. This may not be the 1830s, but Satan has not taken a holiday. We still need to verify before we trust. Is it any wonder that Joseph needed and valued the support and loyalty of men like Orrin Porter Rockwell, Stephen Markam, and others? Joseph clearly understood that he needed to fulfill his mission. He apparently understood that his Heavenly Father could, and likely would, use men like "Old Port" to help keep him safe. So, why would we think today would be any different? Let me give you a thumbnail sketch of the problems during the period of time I served President Kimball.

Today, as in times past, the threat comes from apostates. Yes, the times have changed, but the fundamentals remain the same. Today, the apostates are not as likely to be found among us as they were during the Kirtland period, but there are still some wolves hiding in sheep's clothing, and some, as yet, haven't even discovered their own true natures. We need to remember that Brother Law and others didn't start out as enemies. I'll cover this a little more later in this chapter.

The first thing we are taught in the bodyguard business is the simple fact that there is no one as dangerous as a religious fanatic. There are all kinds of people who pose a threat to others. Probably the most common are those who kill or maim for money. Others never learned to control their emotions; those who were taken over by their tempers, who allowed anger to rule them for a short period, find that by the time their tempers were brought under control, someone was dead or injured. A religious fanatic is a much greater threat than any of the other types, for a host of reasons, the greatest of which is that they generally believe, at least on some level, that what they are trying to do is the will of God. Most of us understand that God works within a set of laws himself, and that he will never tell someone to do something that is out of harmony with those universal laws; however, these people are only interested this pattern when they feel they are being asked to do something that will make them special.

Satan understands that there are men who, because of their incredible vanity, will believe any voice that tells them what they already want to hear. And what they seem to want, above all else, is to live in a spotlight. They want attention; they want to be at the center of their fantasy world. Hence, when a man who operates on this kind of wavelength has a feeling, impression, or vague supposition that looks to make him the big, most important man in his little fantasy world, he will jump on it as his new chief obsession.

These kinds of men cannot be reasoned with, they are not intimidated by laws or law enforcement officers, and they cannot be controlled by fear for their own lives or the lives of their followers. The world of logic and reason has no place in their fantasy world. They almost never lose interest in fulfilling their master plan, and will generally pursue their agenda until they are either successful or dead. It is this fact that makes the security of someone like President Kimball so much more dangerous. The threats aligned toward religious leaders are far worse, in general than those pointed at political leaders. Those who threaten the life of the President of the Church are almost always religious psychopaths, extremists, or lunatics with wild religious fantasies driving their actions. When these kinds of people get it into their heads that the little voices yelling in their brain is God, and that he wants them to murder the president of the Church, nothing will dissuade them from completing that task.

This was the primary reason the Secret Service regional director was so willing to help us with our training. When he and I had our little talk, he took up most of the time trying to enlighten me concerning these threatening men and why they were so much more dangerous than the "garden variety" assassin. While the President of the United States will occasionally deal with the religious fanatic, it is not the norm. But the President of the Church must almost always deal with these mentally deranged types. Religious fanatics constitute a level of danger and lethality far in excess of anything any other kind of assassin can generate.

Up until 1974, the leaders of the Church evidently did not feel a strong impression that any kind of security was needed; but sometime during that year, the Spirit spoke loud and clear that there was now a pressing need that was real and serious. Serious efforts to put together a well-trained, reliable security force designed to protect the president of the Church seemed to come together almost overnight. Not surprisingly, while men on earth were just getting to see the problem, Heavenly Father already had men with special backgrounds already in place, others ready to do the training, and resources standing in the wings.

Satan had made a serious effort to put to death the president of the Lord's Church through a number of homicidal, vain, bloodthirsty killers. Yet, even though we have plenty of evidence that these plans were put into play, they were never successful against the Lord's chosen prophet. There were a number of other leaders of other fundamentalist churches who lost their lives to these mad men, but the assassins were never able to break through the president's security. It is my belief that the security put together during this period of extreme threat was unlike anything the Church has had before or since. Even now, there is an ongoing security force equal to any imminent menace facing the president of the Church. He has his own personal security around him every day, and it would be a simple matter to add to it in any way, should the situation require it.

Disillusioned apostates were the most common enemy during the time I spent with President Kimball. They were generally individuals, or groups of individuals, who broke away and formed their own churches. Let me start with one such group. In Church Security, we began to get intelligence reports about a group who was preaching about taking over the Church. Their plan was to remove the prophet by assassination. We began to get a lot of that kind of information way back in the early seventies. It was just a concern back then, but it was a reason for us to keep our eyes and ears open. Then we began to get word that they were actually murdering one another, fighting for positions of leadership in their own church.

Their own president, Joel LeBaron, was killed by his brother, Ervil LeBaron; at least he was the one who had arranged that killing. Ervil was hoping to become the prophet of their church. As it turned out, the members rejected him in favor of his brother Verlan. So, Verlan was now their prophet, but that put him next in line for assassination. Verlan turned to The Church of Jesus Christ of Latter-day Saints for help and protection. He became our best source of information because he was so fearful of his brother. At this time, we learned a great many things. We learned that Ervil's plan was to remove all the leaders of all the fundamentalist churches, both polygamous and non-polygamous. He planned to take over and consolidate all of the polygamous churches under his church, with him as the prophet and president of all. With the LDS Church and R–LDS (now Community of Christ), he planned to bring them back to the old fundamentalist faith, complete with the practice of polygamy.

Now, while this may seem like a mad man's fantasy, to him it was very real, and he preached that God was helping him achieve it. There might be some thing in what he was preaching, but I am sure it was a different God than we serve. I think it is one truth that even Satan understands—you have got to convince them that they are doing a right thing, even when they know down deep that it is not. The one thing I did learn about Ervil during that period of time was that he was very determined. And to me, he seemed very evil. Looking into Ervil's eyes was a bit like looking into the eyes of Char- lie Manson, and he seemed to have the same kind of control over people. Thinking back on President Cannon's quote earlier in this chapter, it was the eyes of Ervil LeBaron that made the quote come alive for me. He was not Satan, but he was a good clone of him.

Verlan continued to lead the Church of the First Born. The new church formed by Ervil was called the Church of the Lamb of God. With a lot of help from Verlan, we put together a good file on the followers of Ervil, especially the hit men and muscle. They included trained members, at least one brother, and a whole bunch of Ervil's children.

During that period of time, bodies kept stacking up all over Mexico, where the Church of the Lamb of God had its headquarters. In 1974, Ervil and his band launched a raid on the Church of the First Born, hoping to kill his brother Verlan. Verlan wasn't there, but they managed to kill at least two and seriously wounded more than thirteen others. Two more of the leaders in Ervil's church turned up dead that year, clearly at the orders of the leader. Those of us who were in the Church back in the seventies will not have forgotten the assassinations of Dr. Rulon Allred in his office in Midvale. At that point in time, Dr. Rulon Allred (he practiced neuropathy) was the President of the Polygamous Fundamentalist Group known as "The Allred Group."

One of Ervil's wives and one of his stepdaughters simply walked into Dr. Allred's office and shot him to death. An attack had been planned for President Kimball on the same day, but his security was too heavy and they had to call it off. In time, Ervil was arrested and convicted of that killing, and he spent the rest of his life in the Utah State Prison. The rest of his life was not very long; he was said to have had a heart attack a few years later.

During this period of time, I never really dealt with Ervil directly, but one of his little brothers was a real pest. I got to where I could recognize his face in a crowd. From time to time, as we would be traveling to the office or returning home at the end of the day, I would see him in my rearview mirror, trying to sneak up next to our car, presumably to get a good shot. He never got the chance, and I always managed to lose him in traffic. On those occasions when we were playing escape and evasion, President Kimball usually took a nap or worked on a talk. We laughed and called them our white-knuckle moments, which was more true of me than him, I think. I'm not sure his knuckles were ever white. Having said that, I remember a comment he made once that has caused me to wonder. To give you the flavor of this comment let me take a quote from my own journal:

> October 6, 1974. My oldest son, Larry, then a young Aaronic Priesthood holder, had been to Priesthood conference with my son-in-law. While driving the President home, I was telling him about having him there and said I hoped he was proud of his father. President Kimball said, "Tell him for me, if it were not for you, I might be dead by now—you are the one who keeps me alive."

I never quite satisfied myself if that was just a general comment (which was not like him), or if he understood how serious some of those white-knuckle encounters really were. Maybe he understood more about them than I did.

Another group that ought to get a little attention here would be the group called "The Three Davids." While their membership was never as great as the other two just covered, they nevertheless were a major threat. The leadership of this group was made up of some extremely violent and dangerous people. In the beginning, they lead their little group as something of a presidency using their real names. However, as time went on, they seemed to need to inflate their own importance. Referring to a prophecy given concerning the last days, when a great prophet named David would come forth and take over the kingdom of King David of the Old Testament, they started to call their leader David. But the three of them seemed to have a hard time agreeing on just who was in charge, so in time they began to refer to themselves as "The Three Davids." As time went on, even that wasn't enough. In the end, they were teaching that they were the Father, the Son, and the Holy Ghost. Well, no one ever said you had to be sane to start an apostate religion. The one thing they had in common with our old friend Ervil was this strange notion that if they removed the prophet of the Church, they would then become the prophet of the Church. Their top leaders, along with a highly skilled knife assassin, began training themselves to be equal to the task of removing the President of the Church.

They became highly trained as skilled snipers, expert knife fighters, and in the skills of silent assassination such as karate, judo, and jujitsu. All in all, they were a mean little package. Those in law enforcement made it very clear to us not to take these people for granted. They were deadly serious and extremely dangerous. We tried our best to keep good track of them at all times. Anytime any of them were in or around the Wasatch Front, we would be on high alert. This group ended their little reign of terror in the late seventies. Each of the three Davids committed suicide, one at a time. The last made a big news story of his death, because he chose to throw all of his family off of the roof of a Salt Lake City hotel before jumping himself.

With the help of a great many good law enforcement agencies, we were able to keep a good set of files on pretty much everyone who posed some kind of threat to the church or to the President. At the time I served, an Apostle named Gordon B. Hinckley was the General Authority over the intelligence gathering part of our operation. That turned out to be a great blessing for at least two reasons. The first was that he was always the most informed concerning the real threats and he was generally the one briefing the President. The other reason, for me anyway, was that I got to work with him. Not as much as I would have liked, but at least more than I would have otherwise.

Other apostate groups and individuals were constantly being brought to our attention. Some of the other threats included terrorist groups. Generally, these people had no real problem with the Church or its prophet, but both represented serious opportunities to get money or attention, and sometimes both. We tended to encounter these kinds of people when we were on the road or traveling abroad.

During this time, President Kimball's standing orders were, "If I am kidnapped, do not, under any circumstances, try to ransom me!" He saw this as a real possibility and wanted everyone to be prepared for it.

During these years, we also had some pressures from the Black Panthers and the American Indian Movement. These groups didn't necessarily constitute any danger to the President, but we in the President's security were nevertheless aware of these groups.

In addition to the standard groups, there were the individuals. These were generally members who had been caught up in sin, but were so deep into their own personal denial that they would not take any responsibility for their own problems. It has always been amazing to me that when someone is caught in serious sin and gets excommunicated, they want to blame others for their circumstance. During the seventies, there were several different situations where individuals turned their anger on the President of the Church. Each of them were apprehended with one or more guns in their hands, laying in wait to kill the President, simply because they had been excommunicated. As far as I could determine, the President didn't know any of these individuals. Such an action doesn't make sense to the rest of us, but to those who simply cannot admit to any fault, this desperation becomes the only way to shift the blame.

In the last category of threat to the President are those who are mentally operating in a different reality. I don't remember a single General Conference when there was not someone who had to be handled by security because they were totally out of control. Generally, the security people are so well trained that few in the congregation ever realized there was a problem. These people rarely present any threat to the President, but because serious attempts can be disguised in just such a way, we always needed to be sure. Everything had to be treated as a threat until proven otherwise.

It might be easy to look at the death and suicide of so many serious threats and conclude that the threat is gone, but that would be just plain foolishness. Even today, thirty years later, some of Ervil's children are still out there removing names on the list their father gave them. Is our present prophet's name still on that list? Well, I would be astonished if it weren't. And of course that is just one on a long list of threats. I am sure we have added some new ones in the last thirty years. The threat is not going away, at least not until the Millennium. As a Church, we just need to get used to it.

When I agreed to take this assignment, I did not do so as some naïve kid, because I thought it would be a cool job. At that time, I was nearly forty years old. I had been working on the intelligence files, so I knew both the individuals and the groups we would be dealing with. I knew how serious they were and how dangerous the assignment would be. I also knew that somebody needed to take the assignment who knew what he would be getting into. When they asked me, I could see no way to say "pass" and still live with myself.

Very few individuals ever knew what the real level of danger was. I could count them on my fingers: the President's security team, the security administrators, the President, his counselors, D. Arthur Haycock, Gordon B. Hinckley, and maybe a few others who had only bits and pieces. You can be assured that President Kimball did not share the real danger he was in with any of his own family or friends. I know that because, he made it a point to caution me not to divulge anything around them.

1. Wilford Woodruff, *Journal of Discourses* 4:149 http://journalofdiscourses.org
2. Lucy Mack Smith, *History of Joseph Smith by His Mother, Lucy Mack Smith*, (Salt Lake City: Bookcraft).
3. George Q. Cannon, *Life of Joseph the Prophet* (Salt Lake City: Juvenile Instructor, 1888) 430.
4. "Discourse of President George W. Cannon," *Millennial Star*, April 7, 1898.

# 5

---

# The Daily Routine

*"The more clearly we see eternity, the more obvious it becomes that the Lord's work in which we are engaged is one vast and grand work with striking similarities on each side of the veil."*

—Spencer W. Kimball

I'm sure it must seem to the average Church member that the President is always traveling abroad. For President Kimball, the truth was that most of the time, he was working out of his office at the Church Administration Building on 47 East South Temple. And, perhaps not too surprisingly, when working out of his own office, there was generally a rhythm or routine to his life. My average day would start somewhere around five o'clock in the morning. I would then be at the President's residence at five forty-five to relieve the security man who had been on duty during the night. He would pass on any information experienced during his shift, then he would return to the office to log out for the day.

Generally, the President would come to his front door when he was ready, and I would meet him at the door. This was usually sometime between six and six thirty. At the door, I would take his briefcase and help him to the car. After a quick check with dispatch to let them know we were underway, off we would go to the office. We always traveled by different routes; the first rule in protection is never use the same route twice in a row. Never give someone a chance to know your schedule. Never get into a schedule; it makes it way too easy for your enemy.

On my first day with the President, I was still a little unsure about the role he would be playing. After all, he was the Lord's prophet, so I asked him what route I should take. He looked at me, smiled, and said, "Larry, my protection and security is your stewardship. Anything you need to know about protecting me, the Lord will tell you, not me. You just need to listen to the Spirit, then do what it tells you to do. Do that well, and everything will be just fine." Up to that point in time I thought of myself as a fairly good listener where the Holy Ghost was concerned. But from that moment on, I developed a new sensitivity that I didn't even know I had in me. Now, all these many years later, I can say the Spirit never let me down. At those times when I wasn't quite sure what to do, the right course of action just seemed to pop into my mind, and we would get through successfully and smoothly. In addition, I learned more about the principle of stewardship in a few short words from the prophet than I could have in any other way.

When we reached the Church Administration Building area, I would drive into the underground parking lot, pull into President Kimball's space next to the rear door, and then let dispatch know we had arrived. I would then exit the driver side and move to help him out, take his briefcase, and together we would walk down the hall to the elevator. We rode up to the first floor and around the corner to his office. Once there, I would spend some time checking his office, and then I would place his briefcase on the floor next to his chair, and check to see if there was anything else he wanted me to do. Usually that would be a "no." He would sit down and begin working through the pile on his desk. I would go next door into D. Arthur's office and get my orders for the day. Even President Kimball didn't know his schedule as well as Arthur. He was charged with the itinerary, and both President Kimball and I depended on D. Arthur to know what we were going to be doing and when we were going to be doing it. Once I had the day's schedule in my mind, I would go to my desk and get busy on the things I needed to have prepared.

The President's office was in the corner. Next to his office was D. Arthur's office and my desk was in the hall just outside. Like I said before, no one could get to the President's office without first passing my desk and D. Arthur's office. This system insured that there would be no surprise visitors. What if both D. Arthur and I were away? It didn't happen! If the President was in his office, I was at my desk. (The security guy didn't wander.) On those occasions when I was sent on an errand, I arranged to have another member of the team take over my desk. Protection is not about being casual. While at my desk there were a great many things I needed to be getting accomplished. I had to get the security coverage firmed up for the day and week, I also made sure the men were keeping up their training, and I had to keep our intelligence files up to date by making daily calls to all of our information sources, and then making sure the information was passed on to all the members of our team.

On most days, the President tended to work in his office until around lunchtime. If he planned on going anywhere, I needed to have things pre-arranged such as extra men, extra cars, equipment, and so forth. As long as his excursions were already on the schedule, there would be no problem. But, just as things go in all of our lives, unexpected things come up, and where President Kimball's safety was concerned, we did not have the luxury of saying "oh well." Planned or unplanned, it didn't matter, everything still had to be carefully covered. Sometimes the planning had to come together fast, but it still had to be flawless. Something as small as an unplanned haircut had to end up fully planned and carefully engineered.

Even a planned event could cause a problem. For example, almost every day we would load up and drive to the Deseret Gym so the President could get his daily massage from "Nick." As long as the trip to the gym was right on schedule, we had no problem. But on those days when an appointment went longer than their allotted time, we were thrown into a bit of re-vamping. And since President Kimball was not one to cut people off just because they had run out of time, this revamping happened quite often. At the end of his work day (the time he spent in the office), he would gather up the things he was taking home to work on and call me into his office. I would gather up his briefcase, which always weighed a ton, and help him to the car. This was usually around five-thirty or six-thirty.

The trip home might take two or more hours, because we almost always stopped at both major hospitals in Salt Lake City to give blessings to people who were sick or having operations. When we finally reached the President's residence, I would carry his briefcase into the house, say hello to Sister Kimball, see if he needed anything else, and then leave. I would return to the car and wait for the night guy to relieve me. I would then drive back to the office, check with the security control room to see if there was anything in my box, and then head home. On a good day I might be home by seven, but more often it would be closer to midnight. My family got used to seeing me go to bed fairly early because they knew I would be up at five to start it all over again.

Now, that was the description of what I have called an average day. According to my wife, there never was such a thing as an average day. And while I began this chapter by calling it a routine, in truth, it would be hard to really see it as routine. Let's take, for example, the trips to the hospital. They were never on the schedule.

People would call him during the day and plead with him to come and give a blessing to their loved one. Since these were always calls that slipped passed D. Arthur, they were never on the itinerary, so, there was no way I could know what to plan on. I'm not complaining, mind you, because those stops were wonderful experiences to me. Every evening, getting to administer to the sick, partnered up with the prophet of the Lord were, to use Oliver Cowdery's words, "days never to be forgotten." I loved it. Strangely, in all that time, I was never asked to seal the priesthood blessings. I got real good at anointing, however.

You don't have to laugh if you don't think that line deserves a laugh, but I always thought it was funny. Anyway, it was an experience I wouldn't have wanted to have missed. From a security point of view it was always a bit risky—you never want the enemy to figure out your travel route, but when you are stopping at both major hospitals almost every night, it's not hard for them to get your route figured out. Oh well. No one ever promised that it would be easy.

In addition, on any given week, there would be several social events taking place. I felt I needed to be present for those. On the those nights, there would generally be two or more of us. Whenever Sister Kimball would be present, it would require an extra man so neither of them would be without coverage. If other members of the First Presidency would be present, more coverage would be needed. From a security point of view, social events are much harder to cover properly, because the level of control is just not there. Out in a social setting, compared with the checkpoints we had set up in the office, the barriers are only in the skill and training of the security men, at which point it becomes a matter of who is responsible for what space.

With the Secret Service, all of the human resources (agents) are focused on one man: the President of the United States. But in our situation, we may be covering the President of the Church, his wife, and one or more of his counselors. The Secret Service works with a team of a dozen or more agents. We were lucky if we could get three men—total. It always became important to give ourselves a reality check from time to time. The Secret Service was supported by the tax payers of the whole nation. We were supported by the tithing of the members of the Church. We did the best we could with what we had.

Let me digress to make a comment or two about my family. In truth, I was not home nearly as much as I should have been. Sometimes I wondered how my children remembered me from one day to the next. Looking back even now, I feel a huge sense of guilt about that time in my life, but my wife was extremely supportive. She insisted that I do the job to the best of my abilities. I tended to run on about four to six hours of sleep in every twenty-four. But I've got to admit, I loved it! I truly never felt picked on. I really wasn't expected to be there for any more than the normal eight-hour day.

But this was the Prophet of the Lord, and I loved him like I did no one else on earth. I quite simply couldn't trust his life in anyone else's hands.

I understand that is not good leadership, and I suspect that my men felt a little hurt because they must have sensed that I lacked the same level of trust in them that I had for myself. It really wasn't fair of me, because they were truly great guys, and very competent guys, but I just couldn't get it out of my head that it was my watch. President Kimball would not get hurt on my watch, even if I had to sleep on his front steps.

I truly wish I could convey the feelings I had for him, it might help explain the reason for this obsession about my job. There was never a time in my life when I was happier or felt more fulfilled than when I was in the service of the prophet. Just being in the presence of Spencer W. Kimball was thrilling. I felt warm and excited and completely filled with something I can only believe could be called pure joy. I think we have all wondered what it would be like to stand in the presence of the Master. I believe I experienced a small portion of what it must be like by standing in the presence of his prophet. If I am right, then there is one thing of which I am sure: I will never wish to be anywhere else.

When President Kimball said that the Savior was his friend, I am convinced that he did not mean it in some metaphorical sense. The way he talked about his Lord and Master made it clear to me that he knew him as well as he knew me—much better, in fact. President Kimball was also certain that the Savior both knew and loved him as a friend. They were friends who could talk together as one man talks to another, face-to-face. I once asked him the same question about the Apostles. His answer was, "What do you think it means to be a personal witness?" I have always believed that I could come to know more about what the Savior was like from his prophet than I could from any other source.

There is nothing as important as coming to know the Master. To me, it seems, one of the easiest ways to begin that quest is to come to know his prophet. I don't believe you could have been in the presence of President Kimball without coming to sense something of the Lord in him. I know that being in his presence caused me to come to love my Savior more. For me, it was something like an infectious disease you wanted to catch from him and never be cured of. He loved the Master more than any other man I ever met. He loved the Master so much that even serious doubters felt his love, whether they agreed with him or not. I am convinced that Spencer W. Kimball's greatest power was the love he radiated for his Lord and Master. Like John the Baptist meeting with Joseph Smith and Oliver Cowdery, one of President Kimball's biggest concerns was that he not be worshiped. He didn't want to get in between the light of the Master and the people. I loved President Kimball with all my heart, but I tried to never lose track of who we both served. I have always loved my Heavenly Father and his son Jesus Christ, and felt the best way I could serve them both was to offer myself as a tool in their hands to keep their chosen prophet safe.

One of the great questions in the Church, the world, and indeed, the universe is, "Which is more important: the needs of the one or the needs of the many?" When it truly comes down to an either/or choice, the needs of the many must always win out, but as much as possible, the Church has always been about ministering to the needs of the one. As President of the Church, President Kimball always had to wrestle with this issue. People were asking him day and night to come and see to their needs; yet, if he answered all of their requests, there would be quite literally no time left to do the work of the Church. I have already talked about our visits to the various hospitals to bless the sick. Every night, a great deal of his valuable time and energy was spent in that activity. And I learned very quickly that he had little or no skill at saying "no." Now, while we blessed a fairly large number of the sick, I learned it was only a small percentage of the huge number of requests coming into the office. In fact, we were only seeing those who had close enough excess to the President to enable them to bypass his secretary all together.

Understanding that the President could not protect himself, good old D. Arthur was handling the majority of the requests on the side. In a kind but firm way, he explained why the President was not able to personally handle all the requests coming through his office. Without D. Arthur's intervention, we might have been spending eight or ten hours every day just administrating to the sick. D. Arthur would almost always offer a good substitute by finding some other General Authority to fill in for the President. D. Arthur had spent most of his life running interference for other Presidents of the Church.

Needless to say, he had become very good at his job. This showed the great planning and wisdom of the Master. When a man stepped into the office of President of the Church, he might not fully understand what to expect, but there would be an old secretary who had been around for years and knew every problem and success the Church has ever had for the last fifty years. That is a recourse that would be hard to put a value on.

In addition, the Church is not like a major corporation where the CEO or President can be the hard guy everyone expects. The President of the Church can never be a hard guy. He can't get away with giving people answers that they didn't want to hear. Yet, the Church still must be run in some organized way, and sometimes people will not like the answers they get. So, who gets to say no when people want to hear yes? People like D. Arthur try to take that hard role upon themselves as much as they can to save the President from having to get people mad at them.

I have spent a lot of time thinking about how much we, as members of the Church, owe a debt of gratitude to people like D. Arthur. These unsung heroes make sure things run smoothly and rarely, if ever, get any credit for doing so. We all tend to think that our own problems are so important that only the prophet can handle them. If he doesn't see how important our issues are, then he is somehow not the prophet he should be. What we tend to forget is there are thirteen million others who view their issues the very same way.

When I think back on the time I spent with President Kimball, I realize that my favorite time was while we were working out of the office. The main reason for that preference was the priceless time I got to spend with him alone. In order for this make sense, I need to set the stage. Try to imagine yourself alone with the prophet of God for an hour each and every day, free to ask him any question that comes to your mind or may have been on your mind. And then imagine the prophet not only answering your questions, but actually taking time to teach you as well.

At that time in my life, I had a couple of teaching assignments. I was teaching the young adults and the High Priests. That meant that I always had a long list of questions I needed to ask, and he understood he was helping me teach those classes. He never hedged or sidestepped in his answers. He carefully considered each question, and then answered it as clearly and directly as possible. Looking back even now, I can hardly believe it happened. Here I was, a person of little importance, being tutored and taught by the Lord's living prophet. I think it would be important to share one of those conversations, because his response would later turn out to be important to his administration and to the Church.

On one particular morning, we had hardly pulled away from the residence when I asked my question. I had been pondering the question all the night before and was anxious to hear President Kimball's response. "How soon do you think it will be until the priesthood becomes available to all worthy men?" I asked. He responded, "You are right about one thing—it will happen. But I don't expect it to happen in my lifetime." And yet, in June of 1978, about four years after our conversation, it did happen, and he was the one who was presiding when it happened. So, as it turns out, I am one who can attest that while he did not expect it to happen in his time as president, he was concerned about the issue. Yes, he was hoping things would change and was anxious to see those blessings being extended to all worthy men. But I am sure he did not think he was going to be the one to receive the revelation necessary to bring it about.

Over the years, I have tried to stay away from using any of the conversations we had during those years in speaking assignments, classes, or personal conversations with others. First, these experiences were personal to me. Second, but maybe more important, I had no reference for others to turn to. I couldn't just say, "Believe me, because President Kimball told me." It's just my word, don't you see? I needed to be able to say, "If you turn to page 45 in *Faith Precedes the Miracle* . . ." in order to back up my comment. Yet, here I am in this book, making all kinds of statements about how he said this and he said that. Let me just say that I am trying to be careful in making sure that anything I say can be found in one of his books or one of his recorded talks. I promise you, if I didn't have this concern, I could write a whole book just on the conversations we had day after day, riding to and from work.

Some have suggested that President Kimball was not a doctrinalist in his approach to teaching the gospel. He certainly wasn't in the way Joseph Fielding Smith was, but I believe he understood the doctrine just as well as anyone. He had a different approach to teaching it, however. He had a way of simplifying the doctrine so that people would understand it better. Another way he was different, at least in the way I saw him, was he was less likely to let himself feel boxed in by word meanings. He said we need to understand that much of our scripture has undergone some changes because of translation problems.

For example, a word in the King James Bible may not mean precisely in English what it may have meant to the one who wrote it in Hebrew or Aramaic. He believed the only sure source was the Holy Ghost. I guess it would then be unfair to call him a strict doctrinalist. He always advised me to take all my questions to the Lord and then listen to the whisperings of the Spirit. Yet, here I was taking my questions to him. Maybe he was subtlety suggesting I was bothering him too much. I hope not. Most of the time he seemed to be coaxing me to continue asking questions. I always felt he enjoyed our little question and answer sessions as much as I did.

There were a great many things we talked about that I feel I cannot share, simply because there was no verifying witness to confirm the verity of my statements.

Now, while I have made it abundantly clear my reasons for not sharing doctrinal statements, I don't necessarily mean it would be inappropriate for me to talk about experiences or stories. If some of these stories also include some of his attitudes about things religious in nature, just remember: a story is just a story. There is nothing here you need to feel bound by.

A good example of this kind of thing might be my J. Golden Kimball story. I had a question after listening to a speaker during sacrament meeting. It was on a High Council Sunday, and the speaker spent most of his time telling J. Golden Kimball stories. He seemed to be trying for a laugh at the expense of Elder Kimball. His biggest point seemed to be the fact that the language used by Elder Kimball was inappropriate for a General Authority. This talk was very troubling to me, and I could hardly wait for Monday so I could ask President Kimball to help me understand. So, soon after leaving the residence, I blurted out an indelicately worded question: "What do you think about J. Golden Kimball?"

It was a poorly worded question and a really dumb question, in retrospect. His response, however, caused me to spend the rest of the day pondering it, trying to determine what it was he wanted me to learn from it. The first part of his reply was a major message all by itself. He said, "My Uncle Golden"—clearly wanting me to remember we were not just talking about just any General Authority, we were talking about a very special member of his family and someone he knew intimately—"was one of the most spiritual men I ever knew." I must have been expecting a long, drawn out reply, something we would be discussing all the way into the office. Well, that just wasn't President Kimball's style. His answers were generally one or two sentences long. He could say more in one sentence that anyone else I have ever known.

During the next few weeks I researched everything I could find

on J. Golden Kimball and, as I should have expected, found nothing that would countermand or argue with President Kimball's
assessment. While it was true that Uncle Golden did, from time
to time, allow a few "hells" and "damns" to slip into his sermons,
he never uttered a single word that could be construed into something we would call a religious sin, such as using the Lord's name in
vain. And on at least one occasion, when his speaking companion
complained about his bad language, he quickly apologized saying,
"Please forgive me. That was just a little bit of a much larger vocabu-
lary left over from my cowboying days. Not all General Authorities
began their life as a paperboy."

While in this day and age we might look askance at rough language, we need to remember that things were much different back
then. Pretty much the whole church was made up of farmers and
ranchers, and the normal language was a bit more coarse. J. Golden
had been around cowboys, mule-skinners, and hard scrabble ranchers from the time he was a small boy until he was called as a General
Authority. Nevertheless, he was popular among the membership.
President Heber J. Grant said of him, "I always try to get Elder
Kimball as my speaking companion, because I always know he will
draw a large crowd." Farmers and ranchers loved him, because they
said that he was their kind of General Authority.

As I pondered the answer I had received from President Kimball, I began to realize that he was also suggesting that maybe we
put to much emphasis on the wrong things. Just maybe, a little slang
or substandard language doesn't have a lot to do with spirituality.
The one thing I can say, however, is the more I learned about Uncle
Golden, the more I came to like him. President Kimball obviously
knew his uncle Golden extremely well—at least as well as any of us
know our favorite uncles. He believed Uncle Golden was a spiritual
giant, warts and all.

From this and other experiences, I learned that I needed to be
careful not to find fault with someone because they may not fit into
some little standard I have set for myself. Something I may have

thought of as spiritually important may not be all that important to Heavenly Father. It would seem that a large part of what we have come to view as sin can be traced back to the Christian clergy since the time of Constantine at the time of the Great Apostasy. If we really want to get a sense for what the Savior saw as sin, we probably need to find out what the followers of Christ taught before Constantine. President Kimball was intrigued by Section 123 of the Doctrine and Covenants, especially verses seven and twelve. These verses seem to suggest that the early clergy (creeds of the fathers) may have taught doctrines that confused and misled the children of men. Joseph tried to straighten out our misunderstandings, and all of the prophets since his time have tried to do the same.

As we rode together, day after day, I began to get a real sense for how much President Kimball wanted to get us all on the same page. He wanted us to truly come to know the Savior the way he knew him, the real Savior, not the image handed down from the clergy. After all, in a very real sense, the prophet is someone who has a much clearer vision. He has seen God, and his realm, kingdom, and dominion. He has been blessed to kneel at the throne of God, and desperately wants to share that knowledge and experience with us. His biggest task is to find some way to communicate all of that to us. After spending time around President Kimball, I am convinced that this inability to bring us to where they are is the most frustrating thing about being a prophet. I could see it in Spencer W. Kimball, I've read it in the writings of Joseph Smith, and in the writings of all the prophets in between them.

I've spoken with former astronaut Senator Jake Garn. As I looked at him, I thought about how hard it must be for him to try to describe what it was like to look down on the planet Earth. And yet, that would not be the smallest fraction of the difficulty of trying to communicate to us what the sphere of existence where God lives is like. President Kimball would say, "There are simply no words!"

A prophet's job is not so much about telling the future as it is about trying to find some way to introduce us to our Father in

Heaven. It's about describing heaven to us in a way for us to understand what blessings are in store for us, if we can just live up to them. It's about helping us understand what our Father requires of us and why it is so important.

1.  Kimball, *Teachings of Spencer W. Kimball*, 25.

# 6

---

# Spencer, the Man

"I realize I cannot convince you against your will, but I know I can help
you if you will only listen and let me call to your attentions
some salient truths."

—Spencer W. Kimball[1]

Clearly, this whole book is about President Spencer W. Kimball, but I still felt I needed a chapter where I could focus on Spencer, the man. I needed a place were I could talk about the things that made him special and to focus on some things that he seemed to see as important, at least from my point of view.

### Physical Stature

President Lee said of him, "He is the biggest little man I ever knew." He referred to himself as short. My supervisors viewed my size as one of the advantage's I would have as the bodyguard to President Lee. He was a much taller man than President Kimball, and I would have blended in much better alongside President Lee. Next to President Kimball, I looked like something of a fairy tale giant. I worried that the physical discrepancy alone would become a problem. And in some ways, it did. It was much harder for me to look like something other than a bodyguard. But in hindsight, that probably was not as big a problem as my supervisors made it out to be. As far as President Kimball was concerned, he never saw it as a problem. And while he did like to make jokes about his size, I don't believe he saw his size as any real problem. I saw him as a confident man. He had great confidence in himself, and at the same time had great humility—a strange but important blend one does not often see in a man. He was in this way much like Ammon, who believed he could do anything, as long as he was working under God's power. During that first week of working for President Kimball, I made a number of assumptions that proved to be wrong. I understood, for example, that he had been in fragile health for a good many years before assuming the mantel of the Presidency of the Church. So, one of my first assumptions was that I would have no trouble keeping up with him. After all, my greatest power was in my legs. I was half his age and in the best physical condition of my life. Keeping up with him should pose no problem at all. Wrong! For over two years, I struggled to keep within my six foot perimeter. The Lord gave him a new burst of energy; there seems to be no other explanation. There he was, in the last year as an Apostle, hardly able to get around. And then, he is placed under the mantel of God's prophet and proceeded to charge around so fast that he kept me short of breath all the time.

Another part of the same assumption was that he would tire quickly. I got a big surprise here as well. I guess he was always something of a workaholic, and with that new burst of energy, he was right back into his old pattern. I think I was hoping for a normal eight-hour working day, but twelve to thirteen hours was more like it.

### Sense of Cooperation

Before I had even been introduced to him as his security, I had been warned he didn't like the idea of security, so I expected him to make my job a lot harder. Nothing could have been further from the truth, as I experienced it. He was always a pleasure to work with and was always exceptionally cooperative. He would usually ask me how we were going to proceed that day. He would make sure he understood what the security plan was and what would be expected of him, and then he would do his part to help make things run smoothly. I always felt like he and I were working his security as a team. I am sure there are many, even today, who would argue against any idea that he liked his security, but the truth is he did. He did not like the fact that it limited his personal freedoms. He did not like how it complicated and confused those around him. He did not like the fact that it brought people into his life at awkward times and created awkward situations with family and friends.

But others—even his own family—did not fully grasp how clearly President Kimball understood the need for that security. He was brought up to date daily on the security situation. He knew what the real dangers were, both to himself and to those around him. He knew the threats were real and were not to be taken lightly. The intelligence briefings were precise, factual, and certain. Nothing was left out or sugar-coated. These briefings were, in a word, sobering. They were definitely not something you would ever want to share with your loved ones. While he made jokes about how much security messed up his life, he had no questions about why it was needed. As a bodyguard, I could not have hoped for a more cooperative person to protect.

Sister Kimball, on the other hand, did not fully understand the stark realities, nor did she understand how serious the dangers were, even to her. I am not sure anyone, even the President himself, wanted to be the one to share that information with her. We did the very best we could, under the circumstances, to make sure she was safe. And considering the lack of that specific knowledge, she did great. She was a patient individual and put up with all the extra stress we brought into her life. She complained very little, and seemed to take it on faith that security was needed.

**Sense of Humor**

President Kimball's family members describe his sense of humor as self-deprecating, which is sometimes used to suggest self-doubt; this notion would be completely incorrect. He had no problems with his own confidence. In his case, his approach to humor had more to do with his belief that one should never make another person the butt of a joke. By making himself the butt of all of his jokes, no one would ever feel the pain that always comes with being made fun of. For him, all other forms of humor were by their nature an indication of the teller's vanity. In other words, self-effacement is kinder than self-admiration; modestly and unpretentiousness are kinder than vainglorious self-importance. To be perfectly honest, up until that time, my idea of humor had been making a laugh at someone else's expense. His kind of humor had an immediate impression on me. I began to try, from that point on, to follow his example. I wish I could say I have always succeed, but old habits die hard, so the best I can say is that I am still trying.

**Friendship**

Most of us have been around long enough to know the word "friendship" ofttimes has very different meanings for different people. President Kimball understood the true meaning of the word, and he had learned one of life's great secrets about it: "If you are wanting to have a good friend—then, you must first be a good friend." I was working in the temple one day, and in between duties, I was visiting with several of my co-workers. Another of my co-workers sat down next to me and asked, "Why do you spend time visiting when you could be reading your scriptures?" Something President Kimball once said came into my mind in an almost audible way: "There are few things in life more important than developing good relationships." That was not the answer I gave him, however. I simply said, "I read my scriptures every day, at home." President Kimball truly treasured every relationship in his life and worked hard to create new ones. As old adage goes, he not only talked the talk, he walked the walk.

The way he lived his life was always consistent with the things he said. In his life, what you saw was a man dedicated to giving, with little—if any—concern about getting. He had a genuine love for all mankind. He behaved as though he wanted everyone to be his friend; and he would turn you into a friend if you would just give him half a chance. It never ceased to amaze me how people he had met only minutes before thought of themselves as his friends. I believe that he thought of them in the same way. Since he thought of a person as his friend almost immediately, the great law of reciprocation suggests that that person would have little choice but to return that love.

From my point of view, to refer to President Kimball as a friend doesn't even begin to tell the story. To me, he was so much more than a friend. I have referred to him as my surrogate father, but even that is way off the mark. I guess the only thing I can say with certainty is that there simply are no words. So, lets turn to the other side of the relationship and talk about his behavior toward me. I would not presume to read his mind and speak to how he felt about me, but I can say I know he trusted me.

By the very nature of my assignment and the close proximity I was required to keep to President Kimball, much of the business he conducted during any given day took place within my hearing. He and the other Brethren needed to be confident I would never speak of anything I heard outside of that circle of people. I never did and I never will. I tried to always remember that I was just a hired man—something of a menial servant certainly not on par with General Authorities, business executives, or world leaders.

Nevertheless, he treated me with the same deference, respect, and honor that he did these men. You may argue that this is no big thing because he treated everyone that way. But remember, I worked *for* him as a hired man. Do you always treat those under you with precisely the same respect as you show those over you? I will tell you that from my experience, he was not like other men; he clearly did not care about rank or privilege, he was no respecter of persons. Every man was as much his brother as his brother Dell was. Every woman was as much his sister as his sister Clare was.

I believe I can also say with a real sense of certainty that we were friends. I know that he loved me. It really doesn't matter how many people he felt that way about; what matters is that he felt that way about me. Does it really matter that God loves all of His children? No! What really matters is that he does love you.

### Vision and Patience

As we were driving home one afternoon, I remarked that it seemed to me that the prophet Joseph Smith had tried to teach a great many things that the members of the Church didn't seem to understand or incorporate into their lives. His response was short, as usual, but pregnant with meaning. He said, "We"—I understood that to mean "the prophets"—"can only teach the people what they are willing to receive." I found myself pondering that answer for many days after this exchange. In fact, I suppose I am still trying to understand the full significance of that statement. After all of these years, there is one thing of which I am sure: he and all of the prophets of this dispensation know and understand a great deal more than they are able to share with us. It is also clear that the main thing that keeps them from sharing that information is our disbelief. Let me add a little quote from the prophet Joseph to help make this point: "I have tried for a number of years to get the minds of the Saints prepared to receive the things of God; but we frequently see some of them, after suffering all they have for the work of God, will fly to pieces like glass as soon as anything comes that is contrary to their traditions."[2] I believe that each prophet has suffered frustration over our unwillingness to be moved toward God.

Moses tried to bring the children of Israel into the presence of God. Joseph was hoping to do the same, but we are so sure we already know everything that we refuse to listen. I know that President Kimball saw Doctrine and Covenants 123:7 as a very significant verse of scripture. Even today, we still resist the pure knowledge our prophets could share with us because what they know may be in conflict with the teaching of earlier Christian doctrines. Please, let us not forget that our prophets know God, the Reformers only knew *about* Him. We can have a God as man would teach him, or we can have a God as he has revealed himself to his prophets. It is, after all, our choice. But we must be willing to accept what ever they teach us, even if it jars our little world. The Prophet Joseph Smith said, "I could explain a hundred fold more than I ever have of the glories of the kingdoms manifested to me in the vision, were I permitted, and were the people prepared to receive them. The Lord deals with this people as a tender parent with a child, communicating light and intelligence and the knowledge of his ways as they can bear it."[3]

On another occasion, I asked President Kimball what he thought made repenting so hard. I guess it shouldn't come as a surprise that his answer was somewhat long and involved, since he quite literally wrote the book, *The Miracle of Forgiveness*, on the subject. He said, "Repenting is so hard because our pride is so painfully tied up in it." He continued on by pointing out how supremely difficult it is to admit to others that we may have done something that causes us to feel shame. We are being asked to confess to those whose respect we care about that we are flawed, imperfect, and even sinful. He suggested that years of experience had taught him that it seemed even harder for an individual to admit to themselves that they needed to repent. Continuing, he said something I have always thought to be important:

> We have become way too skilled in justifying our own mistakes. One may admit that a thing is wrong, but in their situation, it was somehow different. No matter how serious it might have been, we have created a long list of reasons why we are not really to blame. We were in fact, the victims. Rationalization is just another way of saying the same thing. Today, we might add the word Denial. But his point was these words were the really big disasters of our time, because they keep us from the one thing that could make it all better; which is taking responsibility for our own mistakes so we can truly repent. It is totally impossible for one to repent of something they insist they never did wrong. To repent we must accept the full responsibility for our mistakes. People who think the Atonement will wash away all of their sins are mistaken, if they think they can hide those sins, not confess them, or refuse to accept the responsibility for them. One must truly repent first, then the Atonement will kick in; and in no other way will it work.[4]

This is why President Kimball was so firm on this issue—he understood so well how the process works. He was so intense about the subject of repentance because he knew there was nothing in this mortal experience as critical as our need to repent. The New Testament says anyone who says they are not a sinner is a liar. We are all sinners.

There was only one man who ever lived on this earth who was not a sinner: the Lord Jesus Christ. All of the rest of us are sinners. We may not have sinned today—although that is doubtful—but having sinned even once, we qualify as a sinner. President Kimball said, "We came to this earth to learn how to repent. The scriptures teach, 'There are only two things the angels [those who made it into the Celestial Kingdom, but not into exaltation] envy us [those who do become exalted] for—our ability to repent and our ability to forgive."[5] If this is the critical difference between angels and gods, then we had better be working extremely hard to developing our abilities in these two critical areas.

1. Kimball, *The Teachings of Spencer W. Kimball*, 483.
2. Ibid., 331.
3. B. H. Roberts, *History of the Church of Jesus Christ of Latter-day Saints* (Salt Lake City: Deseret Book, 1902) 5:402.
4. Spencer W. Kimball, *The Miracle of Forgiveness* (Salt Lake City: Bookcraft, 1978).
5. Hugh Nibley, *Approaching Zion* (Salt Lake City: Shadow Mountain, 1989) 301.

# 7

---

# The Counselors

"Jesus knew who he was and why he was here on this planet. That meant he could lead from strength rather than from uncertainty or weakness."

—Spencer W. Kimball[1]

While my assignment was to be the bodyguard for President Spencer W. Kimball, one of the realities of such a task is that he was rarely without one or both of his counselors. Being with him day and night meant being with them almost as much. There is no way I could tell my experience and not include them.

Nathan Eldon Tanner was called to be the first counselor in the First Presidency. He served in the First Presidency to four Presidents of the Church beginning at age sixty-five: David O. McKay, Joseph Fielding Smith, Harold B. Lee, and finally President Kimball. In his earlier years, he had been an oil executive and a government executive in Canada. I remember being told that at one point he was the sixth wealthiest man in Canada. He was the one most responsible for the great Canadian coast to coast pipeline, an amazing feat that provided oil to all of Canada. He had been a major executive most of his adult life and was used to making huge decisions and having them carried out. I don't mind saying that he was quite intimidating to me. It seemed to me that he was always serious. He said very little and smiled even less. President Kimball said of him, "My first counselor is a man of few words, but when he speaks, one had better listen."

In the time that I served President Kimball, I spent a lot of time around President Tanner, so there are a good many things I could say about him. I'll be honest and admit that I was so scared in his presence that I avoided direct contact for the first several months. He seemed to be always there but rarely part of the conversation. When asked a question, he could carry the whole conversation and did so for long periods of time. It seemed to me that he did not offer much unless he was asked. Everything about him was all business. I found myself longing to see him smile. His face seemed like it had been chiseled out of granite. Back in those days, everyone in the Church seemed to know about his past, and it gave him an aura of importance that seemed not to be expressed toward the other Brethren. I supposed that to them, as was the case with me, he was simply intimidating. My problem was that I couldn't avoid him because he was always somewhere within the six-foot perimeter for which I was responsible. So, day after day, we had to deal with each other.

Little by little, we became more comfortable with each other. How grateful I am today for that blessing! As I came to get to know the real N. Eldon Tanner, the cold and intimidating man I thought I knew began to turn into a warm, caring, and gentle man. As President Kimball had so truthfully pointed out, President Tanner was never overly talkative, but when he did say something, his words were always choice. I developed a theory about that aspect of his personality. I recognize that I could easily be wrong, but I think he was just a little shy. (I hope he never gets mad at me for saying that.) All I know is that once he got to know and trust me, he was a totally different man. He was a joy to be around, and I looked forward to any time I was able to spend with him.

To this day I think of President Tanner as a warm, personal friend. However, when in comes to President Tanner, I find I don't have a lot of stories to tell about our time together. As far as I could tell, a sense of humor was not one of the gifts Heavenly Father picked out for him. Laughing together was not one of the things our relationship was known for. Nevertheless, there were a great many things about his character that I tried to incorporate into my own. I wanted to be more like him in special ways. I hope I succeeded a little, at least.

When I think about his contribution to the First Presidency, the word that comes first to my mind is "synergy." He brought talents, skills, and abilities few others had. A First Presidency without an N. Eldon Tanner is hard for me to picture, although I do believe that each First Presidency since has someone special like him onboard.

I cannot make any comment on any other President of the Church, but what I can say about President Kimball is he valued his counselors, and he made few decisions without their input. This Presidency operated in complete unity. Maybe too often we see leaders at the local level who act as though their counselors were simply there to fill out the roster, and that is not Heavenly Father's intentions. A presidency is to operate as one. A good president never goes ahead until he and his counselors are in complete unity on each and every issue. In general, counselors know the role they are to fill. On those rare occasions when one or both counselors start to act as obstructionists, we can be sure that there is a serious problem in that presidency. I believe that I can say without fear of contradiction that this First Presidency was always united. President Kimball had complete and unwavering faith in both of his counselors.

Once I took President and Sister Kimball to a social where the Romneys and the Tanners were also present. The next morning, on our way to the office, the subject turned to Sally Tanner, the wife of President Tanner. I was fairly lavish of my praise of her and spoke of what a special woman she seemed to be. The President smiled and said, "Let me tell you what Sister Tanner taught me." He went on to tell me about a woman he had grown up with in Arizona. She lived a few miles away, but he passed by her place often. Her name was Sally, and she lived in a hovel. Her place was something of a junk yard. Everything one could imagine was scattered from one end of her property to the other. It was all rusted and greasy and nothing but a jumbled mess. Her house was just the same. Sally was just like her house and yard, an unkempt mess. President Kimball said everyone called her "dirty Sally." Although he had not thought about her for years, when he first met Sister Tanner, the contrast came back to him like a lightning bolt. He said, "I realized that I had associated the name 'Sally' with something not truly wholesome. Here was a lady as clean and special as anyone could imagine, and her name was Sally, and I have loved the name ever since." He went on to say that he had gone back in his mind and pondered the woman that he had come to know as "dirty Sally" and realized that his feelings about her had changed, not because he now understood her problems, but it seemed more likely because he had gotten to know a woman named Sally who was such a model of cleanness and refined purity. I remembered in my own life someone we had called "dirty Bill." Thankfully, I had also met a ton of wonderful Bills who were models of unsullied cleanliness. We probably all need to check our past to make sure we haven't attached something unwholesome to a name. People deserve to be known for who they are, not by someone else's name.

Marion George Romney was called in 1941 as an Assistant to the Twelve. He was assigned as the Assistant Manager of the Church Welfare Program shortly thereafter. In 1951, he was called to be an Apostle. Twenty years later, he was called to serve as the second counselor to president Harold B. Lee. President Kimball retained both of President Lee's counselors in the same positions they had served President Lee. President Romney was a great and steady man. He was one who could be counted on to get the job done. Like Sister Kimball, his cousin, he was a product of the colonies. His father had such a flair for getting things done that Camilla said he was the main leader in their colony, even when he had no ecclesiastical position. Marion George was much the same without the flair.

My experience with President Romney was just the opposite of my experience with President Tanner. Not only was I not intimidated by him, but I took to him like son to a long lost father. He was a warm, friendly, lovable person right from day one. He was easy to get to know and easier to like. Like many of the Brethren, he was not at all like his public image. From the pulpit he seemed serious and like a no-nonsense kind of person. Behind the scenes, he was not like that at all. He was someone who loved humor and seemed to never stop having fun with you. He told me so many stories, I have lost track of them.

Yet, he would get me with the punch line every time. I like to think of myself as being too quick to get fooled very often, but he would get me all of the time. The biggest part of his success was the way he told his stories: always with a completely straight face and serious sounding until the last line. Only then did I realize suddenly that he had gotten me again. I don't know how to illustrate this better than to tell you one of his stories. Now remember there is a punch line coming, and I cannot do justice to his wonderful story telling abilities in print, but maybe you will get the idea just the same.

One morning, President and Sister Kimball, George Romney, and I were in the car after a funeral on our way to the cemetery up in the Avenues in Salt Lake City, for those who know the area. The road approaching this cemetery is steep, and at the time it was snowing and covered with ice. All of a sudden, President Romney began talking to me from the back seat. "It was on a day just like this," he said. "I was in the car just behind the hearse. You see that bump in the road just where we are going to turn in? Well, that old hearse hit that bump and the back door of the hearse popped open. President Grant's casket slid out of the hearse and landed in the middle of the road. Well, before any of us could get to the casket, it started sliding down the road. I almost got to it, but I missed.

"There it was," he continued, "racing down this steep road, picking up speed as it went. We were all running down the road, hoping it would slow down, but it just kept racing on faster and faster.

"Now Larry," he said. "You remember what happens to the road when it gets to South Temple?" Then with out waiting, he answered his own question. "It doesn't continue on," he said, smiling. "On the other side of South Temple, at what should be a continuation of the road, there is a drug store, and it is right in line with this road."

By this time I was on pins and needles waiting to find out what had happened to President Grant and his casket. "Well," he went on, "that darn casket slid straight across South Temple and right through the door of that drug store. Still traveling at top speed, it careened across the floor and smacked right into the druggists' counter, whereupon the lid of the casket popped open and President Grant sat up and asked, 'Do you have anything that can stop this coughin'?' "

I probably don't need to add that the most common sound after one of his stories was a groan, rather than a laugh. I remember another time when we were on the way to a cemetery after a funeral, President Romney leaned up from the back seat and asked President Kimball, who was sitting in the passenger side up front that day, "Spencer, do you think they will have ice cream in heaven?" President looked back at him with a bit of puzzlement in his expression and answered, "I don't know." Then President Romney countered, "Well, I'm not sure I want to go, if they don't."

I looked over at President Kimball and saw a slight smile on his face. When it came to President Romney, I always felt like saying to myself, "Got me again." It really never stopped, and you never really knew when it would come next. President Romney just loved life and seemed to need to lighten spirits where ever he went. His life at that time was anything but easy. Sometime before he had almost lost his loving wife, according to President Kimball, he had pled with the Lord not to take her—that he could not go on without her. She lived but was never the same. She required constant care, and he was her caregiver. He cared for her night and day, and it took a great toll on his health and strength. It was mostly because I understood how greatly he needed to find some light and joyful moments in his life that I always tried to set myself up as a target or mark for his stories and jokes. At times his life was so serious that I tried to do all I could to make the way a little more lighthearted and fun. I loved his jokes and the fun-loving side of him. It was always a pleasure to be in his presence.

Like President Kimball, President Romney was demonstrative; having his arm around you was normal and expected. It was sometimes a little challenging for me as security, because he would put his arms through mine as we walked along. This was problematic because I was supposed to keep both hands free to handle any threat that presented itself, which is hard to do when one hand is tied down by the loving tug of one of the ones you are trying to protect. However, I loved the attention way too much to complain or resist. He was so warm and friendly, and he always had time even for just the bodyguard. Like his leader, President Kimball, he was not impressed by rank or title.

President Romney almost seemed to prefer the company of what we sometimes refer to as the little people in terms of self-importance, not in size. I loved him and loved to be near him. One of the first things he ever said to me was, "You from the Uintah Basin Mullinses?" I told him I was, but that I didn't think there were many left out there. "Well," he said, "they were good people." I never did find out who he knew or how he had come to know them. I watched him over time and came to realize he had a gift for remembering people. If any of your family had been in Utah for more than a generation, he probably knew them, which was strange because he grew up in Mexico. I began to notice when meeting him for the first time, people behaved as if they had known him for years. He just had that gift of making people comfortable. In just a few minutes, he knew more about you than people who had known you for years, and he didn't forget. It was one of those things that I have tried to incorporate into my emerging personality. He taught me that if you must talk, talk about the other person. Your part of the conversation should be asking questions about them. At least, that's how he seemed to operate. Still, when I pushed, he would tell me stories about himself.

One of his favorites was about when he and his wife were living near the University of Utah. They moved into a small student flat close to the school. The first night turned out to be a night that would be hard to forget. They woke up in the middle of the night stinging, itching, and covered with their own blood. They stayed awake until morning, when they learned that their rug, furniture, and mattress were infested with bed bugs. He never did say how they overcame the problem, but it didn't seem like an experience I would have liked to have shared. I asked him what he had hoped for as a career, and he said he wanted to "argue the law." He could have said that he wanted to be a lawyer, but it seemed to me that the way he stated it was more honest. I always thought it was a wise thing to have someone with a background in the law as counselor in the first presidency. Decisions concerning the direction that the Church was moving could then be legally considered from the beginning.

1. Kimball, *Teachings of Spencer W. Kimball*, 481.

# 8

## An Equal Partner

"You missionaries go home and find a person that will stimulate you, one that will keep you on your toes. . . . I would never be in the Council of the Twelve today if I had married some [other girl]. Sister Kimball kept me growing and never let me be satisfied with mediocrity."

—Spencer W. Kimball[1]

I chose to borrow the title of this chapter from Edward Kimball's book *Lengthen Your Stride*. It is my plan to look at the word "equal" from a different perspective than Edward did. I want to be clear: I am not taking issue with the way he meant the words to be taken. I simply mean I would like to look at the meaning of the phrase, "equal partner" in a different way. Generally, when we use the word "equal," we mean "at the same level," or "just as valuable as." If we are talking about a married couple, as in the case of President and Sister Kimball, we would mean that President Kimball saw Sister Kimball as being just as important to him as he was to himself. Her needs, desires, and hopes would be just as important as his needs, desires, and hopes. Her comforts would be just as important. From my observations alone, saying he saw her as an equal would be incorrect. Why would I say that? Because to President Kimball, his wife's needs were a good deal more important. Her value to him transcended any concern he had for himself. At the time in his life when I walked in his shadow, everything I saw and everything he said attested to the fact that he believed that her needs, comforts, pleasures, and desires were a higher priority in his mind than his own. He himself might have used the word equal to describe their relationship, but the fact that he valued her feelings above his own was attested to each and every day.

For one thing, he always made sure she was well taken care of and was much more concerned about her well-being than he was about himself. I don't think a day ever went by that he didn't ask me to check to make sure everything was being done to see to her needs. His concern for himself was almost nonexistent, but his concern for her seemed to be always on his mind. He loved her in a way that entirely overwhelmed and erased his self-interests.

At first glance, one would think a book about the experiences of the bodyguard of the President of the Church would be about the bodyguard and the President, but my real life experience covered so much more. For example, would it really be possible to cover the President and not cover his partner? First of all, for a large part of the time, they would be together. Also, anyone who wishes to harm someone clearly understands that to harm those closest to him can usually do the target more damage. Protection, then, for Spencer W. Kimball always included protection for Camilla Eyring Kimball.

I wish I could say that she was always covered as fully as she should have been, but she was not. I wish I could say that he was covered as fully as he should have been but that would not have been the case either. I can say that we (the security team assigned to him) tried to cover both of them to the very best of our abilities, using all of the resources we had available. Someone once said, "Work as if everything depended on you, and pray as if everything depended on the Lord." We always understood that the Lord carried almost the whole load. We also understood that the Lord counted on us to be ready to serve him as tools in his hand. A Secret Service agent once asked me how I felt I could do this job with the few meager resources available to me. I wondered how he thought he could protect the President of the United States without the Lord calling the shots. I always wanted to do better and to have more resources with which to do the job, but I always had faith that the Lord was orchestrating our efforts, and making sure that everything went as he wanted it to go. But we still worked as though everything depended on us. I can say, without fear of being contradicted, that all of my supervisors in security got extremely tired of my constant whining for more, more, more.

It often happened that because Sister Kimball was going to be doing something we had not counted on, we would need another man, another car, or another radio. I fully understand what a big pain I was, but I was not about to let anything happen to her. I rarely got what I requested, but that came as no surprise. Security was a relatively small department with a limited budget and even fewer men to cover all the security needs. But just in case anyone should get the idea that she was the cause of any of this, she wasn't. Just the opposite was the case. Sister Kimball did not want any fuss made over her. She would have been the happiest if security would have left her alone, but our job was to protect her and to make sure no harm could or would come to her.

You will never know how hard it was to sell her on that notion. It took time, patience, and a lot of love, and even then she still didn't like it, but she would live with it, but only if the men providing her security were men she knew and trusted. This is one of the things the security control room never seemed to get. "We'll just send you Brother So-and-so," they would say. Her response was kind of, "I don't think so!" More than once, I had to send another member of our team with President Kimball so that Brother Peart or I could go with her. Was this the right way to handle these sorts of situations? Yes. This is the way President Kimball wanted it, and it was more than just a little important that she be comfortable.

Only those closest to President Kimball understood how very crucial she was to him and thereby the Presidency. Almost his whole effectiveness as the President of the Church depended on her. His love for her was complete. I don't believe that he had any fears for himself, but he would often make serious extra efforts just to make sure that I had her well protected. She, of course, would tell me nothing about her needs or schedule, but he would take me aside and tell me she was planning to go shopping, to a speaking engagement, or to some other thing and he would say, "Larry, could you see to it that someone go with her and watch over her?"

Whenever possible, I assigned that duty to myself. I just loved being around her and took every chance I could to be there. I would like to go on record as one who is proud to proclaim to the Church and world that this was the most special woman who has ever lived on this earth. She was, by nature, a little shy, and unassuming. I believe that she was comfortable standing in the shadows of her husband. I have always felt that it was a something of a shame, because the Church never got to know her and how special she really was.

I always felt a little guilty because her children had to share her with me, and I wasn't even able to ask their permission. One of the reasons I got to know her so well was a planned response to a regular problem. Usually when we got out of the car or out of an activity, members of the Church would rush to the President, as if he were some great magnet. They were usually there as families. It always seemed that the leader wanted to show his family or the other members of his group that he could sway or prevail the prophet to come with him to be introduced to his group. I was never quite sure about the motives behind those push and shove matches.

Regardless, the throngs tended to separate the President from his beloved wife. She would be left standing all alone. That would disturb me from at least two different perspectives. First, she would be all by herself without any security. More important, she was left feeling hurt, abandoned, and cast off by otherwise good members of the Church who, in their zeal, had neglected her.

So it became standard procedure (with the President's approval) that I turned his protection over to the Number 2 man, and I went over to her side. My intention was to try to distract her, somehow help her forget the hurt she was feeling, and get her mind on more pleasant things, usually by getting her to talk about her childhood in the Mexican colonies. This stratagem produced two rewards: first and most important, it was such a happy memory that it totally filled her mind and caused her to forget feeling neglected. Second, and important only to me, I got to know her and what life in the colonies was like. While I have never been to colonial Juarez, I feel like I know what life was like there before the revolution.

For me there was nothing to compare with getting to know her. From my perspective at least, she became my friend. I think that I kind of saw her as a surrogate mother, but I'm sure that idea would not have appealed to her. She would have been most comfortable with the idea of our being friends. So we talked about the colonies. She loved growing up there. She always called her childhood home "the present day Garden of Eden." She was a grand woman. I have never met another that even comes close to being as wonderful as she was. That year, as her birthday approached, her family determined to throw a special party for her. It would be her eightieth birthday, and clearly something special was in order. It was decided that her party would be held in the Church Administrative Building. It was to be a large gathering and was to be all family. A few days before, she took me aside and asked me if I would come to her party. I told her not to worry—I would be there as security.

"No, no," she said. "I want you to be there as my guest." Now this invitation was awkward for several reasons. First, it had been made abundantly clear that the guests were to be all family. I knew that even if I did come as a guest, I would be out of place, and other family members might be a little offended. In addition, I was the commander of President Kimball's security. I was expected to provide leadership for all the security needed for that event. Still, I could never manage to say no to her, for this or for anything else. In the end, I managed to put together enough security to cover everything with me out of the picture. I drove President and Sister Kimball to the party, dropped out of my security role, and did my best to assume my guest role.

As I had previously expected, it was pretty uncomfortable. The highlight for me that night was that there was another person that was there as a guest who was not family, but an old family friend. He was an FBI agent named John (as I recall). His presence took a little of the pressure off and made things just a little less awkward. Even so, the other members of our security team gave me a hard time for days after that. It was a hard experience, but just the fact that Sister Kimball had wanted me to come to the party as her guest made it all worthwhile. In hindsight, however, it has become clear to me that it was things like this that began to be my undoing with my bosses in the security department.

A few years ago, I was asked to do a fireside on Camilla Eyring Kimball in Green River Wyoming. I was able to take the whole hour telling stories about her life in the colonies, which was alright for me to do even back then. While I was telling stories about her, I had strong impression that Sister Kimball was sitting in the front row. By that time, she had been long gone from this mortal experience, and residing in the spirit world. I was both stunned and astounded; needless to say, this impression brought my presentation to a halt for what seemed like a long time. Then, choking down my emotions like her nephew Hal (that would be President Henry B. Eyring today) so often does, I was able to continue. I add this story here simply to point out she asked me to be her guest at her birthday party, and then she got to be my guest at a fireside her honor.

Sister Kimball was a great lady—not in some superficial way, but in a deep, substantial way. She was a voracious reader. I can hardly think of her without seeing a book in her hand. Whenever we traveled anywhere, she always took a number of books. No one knows that better than I do, because I always ended up carrying most of them, at one time or another. Now, if in your mental picture, you see only scriptures and Church books, you would be wrong. As a reader she had very eclectic tastes. She seemed to want to know about everything. She was, perhaps because of her constant self-education, a very articulate and eloquent conversationalist.

Sister Kimball was a joy to talk to. She could speak on any subject presented into the conversation. It was a bit strange to me—as I sat back in my shadow position watching, several people would be in deep conversation on a subject that I knew because of my conversations with her. Yet she would sit quietly in the background and not even enter into the conversation. I can't say that I ever figured all that out, but I'm guessing that she felt free to talk only when she felt others in the group respected her views or opinions. This is so unfortunate, because she was a person everyone ought to have known and appreciated.

As I have already suggested, President Kimball would often ask me to see to it that she be protected for one thing or another. If he was going to be staying in his office, or if I could assign someone else to cover him, I would assign myself to her. Sometimes it was nothing more than taking her shopping or occasionally to the laundry. It was great fun to sit and talk to her. What I really liked to do was just listen, but she would not have that—if you wanted her input, you had to be willing to carry your side of the conversation.

I want to share one other thing about Camilla that the members of the Church don't know. During the Kimballs' lifetime it may have been a bit too personal for them to talk about, but now I think it is alright for me, someone on the other side, to share. That subject is Mary, Camilla's younger sister by about four years. Mary was born deaf. For a short period of time, Mary was sent to a school for the deaf, but the family was very poor, so their father asked Camilla to take responsibility for Mary. For a large part of her life, Mary lived with Camilla. Camilla accomplished many wonderful things as a young lady, which are made more even more impressive when one considers that she did most of those things with Mary as an added burden. Maybe I was a bit more sensitive to this because my grandmother on my paternal side had a similar challenge in her life. As a young woman, her father made her promise to be the caregiver for her younger sister who was mentally handicapped. I have seen firsthand the sacrifices required to fulfill such a promise. For Camilla, her responsibility for Mary was pretty much a lifetime commitment. In some ways, Mary was as much a responsibility for President

Kimball as his children were. The big difference was his children all got married and moved out. Mary was there until the end.

I must admit it is hard for me to stop talking about Sister Kimball. I know so many wonderful stories about her, especially her days as a young woman. I could write a book on her alone, but her youngest son Eddy (I know he likes to be called Edward, but his mother always referred to him as Eddy) has written a wonderful book entitled simply *Camilla*. I must say, in closing this chapter, that there are a great many wonderful stories about her that still need to be told.

Let me tell you a little I learned about Camilla. She always said her childhood was rather normal and unspectacular, and I am sure that it seemed that way to her. She was the oldest child in the family. Oldest children generally find that they were called on to grow up a bit faster than the others, because they needed to help Mother get the chores done. I'm sure that was the case with Camilla. When she was in her mid-teens however, something began to happen that would terrify most teenagers today. A war began to ferment. Her young life was filled with a great deal of fear and concern about her family's safety. After a lot of posting back and forth, the people of the Mormon colonies knew that their time of peace and safety was over, and they were being pushed out of Mexico—all they had ever known as home.

An interesting thing about Camilla that most people don't know is that she was very involved in helping her father in the roundup of his cattle. Out of all of his children, Camilla was the best on a horse. Nevertheless, when it came time for the women and children to leave, she had to go with them. She would have liked to stay and help her father with the cattle. Besides being a great hand with the cattle and quite proficient in the saddle, she also learned to ride a motorcycle soon after they hit the market. She was always ladylike but with an adventurous streak not seen in women in her day. She was even a bit embarrassed to talk about such things. In my opinion she did not fit any mold other than her own.

Another story told in the family centered around the time she went off to study at the University of California at Berkeley. She spent what little money she had for schooling and her room and board. One source of information insisted that she be able to bring her sister Mary with her. Anyway, Camilla didn't have enough money to buy the food they needed to stay fed from day to day. It was 1915 and the International Exposition in San Francisco (also called the World Fair) was in full swing just across the bay. So she and Mary spent a day once a week going through the food booths filling their handbags with samples. Then at the end of the day, they would return home with enough food to get through the following week. That was the kind of independent, creative, and brave person she was.

While she was quite comfortable with a role where the attention was on her husband rather than on herself, I always felt it was regrettable that the members of the Church never go to know this remarkable woman. In my opinion, there was never another woman like her and the world is a poorer place without her. To this day, I am still not quite sure how to describe her. She stands somewhere in between a surrogate mother and a great friend.

1. Kimball, *Teachings of Spencer W. Kimball*, 303.

# 9

---

# The Majordomo

"If you don't have the Brethren's total confidence, if they can't talk about anything or anyone, any situation or circumstance with you sitting there, it doesn't work."

—D. Arthur Haycock[1]

While this book is, and rightly should be, about President Spencer W. Kimball, I cannot and should not ignore the huge contributions made by his personal secretary, David Arthur Haycock. I have little doubt that President Kimball would have found a way to be successful on his own, but having someone with the background and skill of D. Arthur made his work and his life a great deal easier.

As a high school student, D. Arthur made up his mind he wanted to be some kind of secretary. Over the next two years, he enrolled in classes in shorthand to improve his skills. It has always been amazing to me how a little decision like that can set the course for your whole future. This decision, however, may have been influenced by the fact that, as a child, D. Arthur received a severe burn that affected his ability to do serious physical things.

While he was serving as a missionary in Hawaii, he made the next major life decision. President Heber J. Grant made a tour of the mission, and D. Arthur was able to spend some time with him and his party. One of those along with President Grant was his personal secretary, Joseph Anderson. D. Arthur was very impressed with Brother Anderson and the way he served President Grant. He made the decision right then that he wanted to spend his life doing the same thing. He served as the secretary and stenographer in the mission home, and came to enjoy the task of coordinating and organizing things in the mission, which confirmed this decision was right for him. He was released from his mission in 1937 and promptly married his childhood sweetheart Maurine McClellan in the Salt Lake Temple. D. Arthur was not the kind of person who spends a lot of time waiting for life to come to him. He set off right away trying to make his dreams come true.

He took a job in the Church Finance Department. Because of World War II, he had to leave Church employment for a short while. During this period of time, he worked with a young man named Gordon B. Hinckley, but as soon as the war ended, he returned to Church employment. While he did not work as the personal secretary for President Grant, he did work on the same floor and was able to get to know President Grant very well, talking to him almost every day.

After the death of President Grant, President George Albert Smith became the next President of the Church. At first, Joseph Anderson served as both the personal secretary and the secretary to the First Presidency. D. Arthur was made his assistant. After a short period of time, D. Arthur was assigned as the personal secretary to President Smith and Joseph Anderson the secretary to the First Presidency. They worked together as a team from that point on. President Smith seemed to enjoy having someone to talk to, and D. Arthur was wise enough to understand the value of listening to a prophet of God. When D. Arthur felt like talking to me in that same manner, it was usually about George Albert Smith, presumably because no one had shared more about himself as had President Smith, or maybe he was just D. Arthur's favorite. All I know is, I heard so many stories about President George Albert (D. Arthur usually left off "Smith") that I came to feel I really knew him.

In April 1951, the Presidency again changed hands. The new President was David O. McKay. President McKay did not choose D. Arthur as his personal secretary. For a time, D. Arthur served under Joseph Anderson as the assistant secretary to the First Presidency. In 1952, Dwight D. Eisenhower became the President of the United States of America, and he made Ezra Taft Benson his Secretary of Agriculture. Elder Benson asked D. Arthur to accompany him to

Washington as his secretary. He did so. He served with President Benson until 1954, when D. Arthur was called to preside over the Hawaiian Mission. In 1958, he was released after serving four years. He had no sooner returned to Salt Lake City when he was asked to become the executive secretary to the missionary committee.

In 1970, President McKay died and D. Arthur was asked to return and resume his position as personal secretary to President Joseph Fielding Smith. At the time he (President Smith) became the president of the Church, he was ninety-three. No one had ever become the president at such an advanced age.

D. Arthur and President Smith developed a close personal relationship. President Smith passed away in 1972, and again D. Arthur was asked to serve President Harold B. Lee as his personal secretary. President Lee passed away in 1973, and D. Arthur was again asked to stay on as the personal secretary to President Spencer W. Kimball.

Now, after all of this, I believe it is exceedingly clear why I would suggest that no one could have been better prepared to serve as the personal secretary to President Kimball and also why I would suggest that he had, by now, learned pretty much all there was to know about running a Presidency. The Lord, in his great wisdom, seems to have planned it that way. Every new president comes into that office not fully understanding what being the president would entail. President Kimball once joked to his family, "If I would have known how hard this was going to be, I wouldn't have run for the office."

D. Arthur was the key to keeping things running on an even keel while the new president got in step. After serving pretty much his whole life as the personal secretary to the president, he understood what was expected.

When I decided to entitle this chapter "Majordomo," it was with a full understanding that in Great Britain, it is a term most folks are well acquainted with, while people in the U.S. might be less familiar with the term. The majordomo is generally someone who runs an estate. He is more than a secretary, a manager, or a simple steward. The majordomo is, in fact, more like a lord chamberlain or someone who runs a large hotel—a *maitre d' hôtel*, if you will. If you remember the old TV series *Magnum PI* starring the young Tom Selleck, there was an English gentleman named Higgins who was just such a man. I use the term affectionately for D. Arthur; he was in all respects a majordomo, but a very lovable one. He ran everything as smoothly as a fine-tuned watch. And every Prophet he served loved him for it.

In every leadership role there comes a time when the boss has to say no. While this concept is generally understood in the work world, in the world of religion too many seem to be just laying in wait, hoping to find a good excuse for turning away from the Church to a life that is easier and less demanding. It is quite difficult for a prophet to ever seem to be anything less than perfect. And in a one-on-one situation this usually means that the individual believes, "The prophet will never disagree with me."

Understanding how all that works, D. Arthur was ready to step in and play the bad guy when needed from time to time. For example, requests came into the office every day from groups, wards, stakes, and individuals who wanted President Kimball to come and speak at some special function or another. Truly, there wouldn't be time enough to speak all day, every day, but how does the President of the Church say no? Well, he doesn't—D. Arthur does.

In Chapter Five, I talked about how often President Kimball went to hospitals around the valley to give blessings. While we spent quite a bit of time each and every day answering requests, I can't possibly imagine what it would have been like without D. Arthur running interference on 90 percent of the actual requests coming into the office. Someone had to be there to reserve some of the prophet's strength and energy for the task of running the affairs of the Church. It irritated me to think that people were so focused on themselves and their needs that they never seemed to even think about the President's needs or health.

Perhaps people equate a "personal secretary" with someone who writes letters and takes shorthand. Well, I can state from personal experience that those were just the smallest parts of what D. Arthur did day after day. D. Arthur ran everything—certainly under the direction of President

Kimball, but under his support as well. People would say that President Kimball was my boss as well, but it seemed more like I was receiving my orders from Arthur. Let me try to explain it this way: while the President and I had a comfortable relationship, he never gave me orders nor did he really even give me direction. D. Arthur did all of that.

It was kind of like working for a kind, tolerant, aging father, but having an older brother as your direct-up-the-line supervisor. I understood that President Kimball was my ultimate boss, but I turned to D. Arthur for direction. I've had a lot of bosses in my long lifetime, but I never had one as gifted as D. Arthur. I really looked forward to being supervised by him. I always felt like he was my greatest supporter. He made me feel like we were a team.

D. Arthur was not a big man nor was he a powerfully strong man. Yet, his first priority was to protect the president of the Church. I believe D. Arthur saw me as the physically strong body he could use to accomplish his goal. I became the strong arm of D. Arthur himself. We became such a great team because he felt he was accomplishing his chief desires through me and the security team. By definition, we were a team because we had the same goal and the same purpose— that of ensuring the safety, health, and protection of the President of the Church. I think D. Arthur questioned the real intents of many good members when it came to what was good for the President. I saw good members who seemed willing to put the President under physical strain when it served their interests.

As I am sure you can imagine, when you are directly attached to the president of the Church, you will of necessity, spend a lot of your time working while he is meeting one on one with special people like presidents of other countries, highly placed governmental leaders, leaders of other churches, and dignitaries of one thing or another. Most of the time, it was D. Arthur and me among these great men and women.

It turned out that D. Arthur was one of the all time great storytellers. All of his stories were true, and if that weren't good enough, all of his stories were about former Presidents of the Church. He would start out: "Let me tell you a story about President McKay." And then I would be treated to some wonderful story that would always cause me to come to love President McKay even more. One thing I realized right away was that the more I learned about these men, the more I came to see their human, mortal side, the easier my love flowed toward them. Prior to that time, I thought of a prophet as someone not really human, someone who had already been translated and was already perfect. I began to see that even they were here to take this mortal test just like the rest of us. My experience with President Kimball taught me that by the time he was called to be the prophet, he had progressed so far in his life that he was able to converse with the Master face-to-face without compromising or invalidating his mortal test. And so it was with each of the presidents of the Church. By the time they had reached that point in their lives where they were to take on the mantle of authority, they had already passed their test, both in the sense of going beyond and also in the sense of successful completion.

While interviewing President Gordon B. Hinckley, television personality Mike Wallace suggested that there was something wrong with having old men lead the Church, whereupon President Hinckley replied, "Isn't that wonderful!" He talked about the value of having seasoned, mature men lead the Church. It is proof of God's wisdom that the Presidents of the Church are men old enough to have been involved in working out their salvation for many years, and that by the time they are called to lead the Church, they have proven themselves to God, to the Church, and maybe most important of all, to themselves. No one but a fool would agree to take the helm of this ship without full confidence that God was with him and that God approved of him, and that he could count on God to direct him in every decision. In the experience of D. Arthur Haycock, four of the Presidents of the Church were very different in terms of their personality and character, but very much the same in their love of and obedience to God and his commandments.

One of the problems in this area is that for the average member of the Church, we know well one or, at most, two presidents. That is a shame, because our testimony is so strengthened when we get to know more. For example, President Kimball was so kind, gentle, loving, and patient, and yet, nothing got missed on his watch. One would never think if him as hard-nosed, but nothing got by him, and the Church moved ahead in leaps and bounds. President Lee, on the other hand, was more businesslike and serious and seemed to have endless energy. His time at the wheel was just as successful. President Joseph Fielding Smith was a little harder to figure from the outside. At the pulpit, he was all seriousness. Many members thought of him as harsh and maybe even a little cold—the truth, however, was different. Out of the public eye, he was almost the opposite. He was warm, soft, gentle, kind, and forgiving.

President McKay was a bit more like President Lee—pretty much a serious business man. In public and at the pulpit, he seemed the most patient and forgiving of men, but behind the scenes, he was stickler for perfection. Many tales have been told of administrators who returned again and again with an assignment or report until they got it right. He would take his red pencil and correct even the smallest of errors. One got to turn in his assignment only when it approached perfect. Yet, the public perception was also accurate: although something of a perfectionist, he was still loving and kind—he was someone anyone would love to have as a grandfather.

But it always seemed to me that D. Arthur told a great many more stories about President George Albert Smith then all the others put together. D. Arthur clearly had a special love for the president he always referred to as "George Albert." And George Albert was clearly a very curious individual whose out-of-the-public-eye image was extremely different than his public persona. As a young man, his eyesight was so poor that by today's standard, he would have been labeled as legally blind. D. Arthur said the lens in his spectacles were as thick as the bottoms of a couple of coke bottles. And yet, even as a youth, he had trained himself to be such a great performer that even the General Authorities would ask if some of their meetings could be ended early so they could go catch one of George Albert's one man shows. In his one man show, he generally sang the popular songs of the day, played six different musical instruments, and did a lot of what we would call today as "stand-up comedy."

Now I don't want you to get the idea that D. Arthur stories were only about the presidents he had served. He told many other stories about other General Authorities, but only the things he had personally experienced. It was a wonderful education for me; I suspect D. Arthur liked telling those stories as well. Maybe one of the most important things I learned from these stories was a glimpse of some of our Heavenly Father's hopes for us. He is an exalted being, and he hopes we will follow him and become exalted beings ourselves. But he is not trying to turn us into little clones. He wants us to develop personalities of our own. He wants us to retain our individuality, but there are certain principles we need to internalize to gain a fulness of joy and happiness. If we fail to understand and internalize these principles, we will never be able to gain that fulness. We don't have to be alike; in fact, God loves diversity, but always within the principles of righteousness. The more you come to know the Brethren, the leaders, the General Authorities of the Church, the more you will see the diversity among them—but always there will be unity as to their righteousness.

Few others in the Church have seen the true nature of these men. D. Arthur's stories reflected his testimony that they were all men of God. Each in his own way struggled to do the will of the Father. They stumbled from time to time, but each held firm in the knowledge that they were disciples of Christ and that he was with them to help them up, dust them off, and lead them again to the path toward the final goal of exaltation. He is also there for each of us, if we will just have faith in him.

1. Heidi S. Swinton, *In the Company of Prophets* (Salt Lake City: Deseret Book) viii.

# 10

---

# The Others

"Let him contend earnestly for the redemption of the First Presidency of my Church, saith the Lord . . . and his sacrifice shall be more sacred unto me than his increase, saith the Lord."

—DOCTRINE AND COVENANTS 117:13

In addition to D. Arthur Haycock, there were a number of other individuals who made up a group whose job it was to support the President of the Church and the First Presidency. First among them would be Brother Francis M. Gibbons, the secretary to the First Presidency. While their assignments were different, it was always amazing to me how smoothly D. Arthur and Brother Gibbons got their jobs done as a team. They had been good friends for a long time, and were used to working together. In addition, Brother Gibbons had an assistant whose name was Frank Michael Watson. They were both involved in everything we did. For me, this became the team surrounding my President, so it made perfect sense that they also became my friends. While I got to spend time almost every day talking to Brother Gibbons, I can't say we became close personal friends, but we were good friends, and I truly enjoyed the time I spent with him. He was a wonderful man, and I truly wish I could have gotten to know him better.

Here's one little anecdote on Brother Gibbons: as I have stated earlier, I was teaching a couple of classes as part of my Church callings. Like every other teacher, I had a great many questions asked that I was not always able to answer with confidence. My students couldn't be told how I spent my work days, so I had to get answers for them without raising more questions as to the nature of my sources.

I learned that Brother Gibbons seemed to always know the answer to the question of the week, and I got used to turning to him whenever I could. I have always had a pet peeve with teachers. When asked a question that they don't know the answer, they tend to react in one of two ways. Either they fake an answer, and the class always seems to know when they do that, or they say, "I'll get back to you on that," and then never do. Well, thanks to the wonderful resources surrounding me every day, I was always able to bring back the answer to the question.

Now, when it came to Brother Gibbons's assistant, F. Michael Watson, things were a little different. We were closer to the same age and we hit it off much better. I really loved talking with him. He was warm and friendly, always serious and professional, but easy to be around. I felt we had a much more comfortable relationship. I can truly say I shared things with him I have shared with few others. He and Brother Gene R. Cook, who was at that time the secretary to the Seventies, used to meet every day for lunch at the high rise cafeteria. Some other members of the President's security team would join in from time to time. These were times to remember. Here were two wonderful men who were special because they had the Church at the center of their lives.

There is something unique about discussions that center on the things of true importance. In this life, so much time is wasted talking about things of no or little importance. "Who won the game?" "Did you see the new movie?" "Who is your favorite singer?" You know, real important things like that. Well, our conversations with Brother Watson and Brother Cook centered on things like "Why is it important to really know God?" "How does one get to really know him?" "Why is it important to overcome the world?" "What do you have to do to overcome the world?" These were special times, as Oliver Cowdery stated, never to be forgotten. These two names will not be unfamiliar to the reader; Brother Cook went on to become a Seventy. F. Michael became the secretary to the First Presidency until 2008, when he was also made a Seventy. Most of those in and around the

Church Administration Building referred to him as "Mike." A few of us, in a fun-loving way, sometimes called him "Frank" because we knew he preferred Mike. He was and is a wonderful man, and I treasure the relationship we once had.

Another fixture at the Administration Building was Gordon Afleck, who's job, as near as I could understand it, was the building itself. He was responsible for pretty much everything from assigning office space to office socials. When it came to 47 East South Temple, D. Arthur Haycock, Francis M. Gibbons, F. Michael Watson, and Gordon Afleck were the organizing force. Someone wisely said, "It's not the Boss, it's the Boss's secretary who really runs the show." With Church Administration that's not entirely true, but there were some areas where that statement is not far off. Nevertheless, way back behind the scenes, these four men deserve a great deal of gratitude for how smoothly things always came off.

While I am talking about support people, let's leave the Administration Building, and travel to Deseret Gym. Almost every day, I would load President Kimball up for his daily trip to see Nick. I never came to know anymore of his name than that, just Nick. Nick was the man who gave President Kimball his daily massage. Back when he was dealing with so much in the way of health problems, President Kimball's health providers found that he benefited from a daily massage, especially in terms of stress relief. When he became the President of the Church, these massages seemed to again make a real difference in his ability to handle the pressure. President Kimball referred to him as "Nick with the magic hands." He had been previously cleared by our security people, so I wasn't involved in getting to know him as I might have if I had done the clearance, but I got to know him man to man, and I trusted him enough that I felt I could leave them alone from time to time if I needed to.

While I am on the subject of his health, let me tell you a story concerning Dr. Russell M. Nelson. I know he is Elder Nelson of the Quorum of the Twelve now, but back then he was Dr. Nelson. One afternoon, on the way home from the office, President Kimball asked me to take him to a school near his home, so he could vote. Sister Kimball had already voted earlier in the afternoon. We made the little side trip, and I took him in to vote. There was a long line, and as soon as people saw who it was, they tried to move aside to encourage him to move to the head of the line. Anyone who really knew him would know that was just not his style. Clearly he would have no part in having others move out of the way just so he could move in front of them. He took his place at the end of the line and began patiently waiting for his turn.

Standing in line in front of the President of the Church clearly made most there very uncomfortable, but he was unwavering in his determination to take his proper turn. It really was a long line, and the voting was taking a long time. I started to notice that President Kimball was not looking his normal chipper self. He seemed to be loosing some of is natural color. I got into a position where I could see him really up close and studied him for signs of weakness. About that time, he came to the voting table and got his ballot. He went into the booth and voted. As soon as he came out, I could see he was not looking good at all, so I called for a little help from the voting officials, and we found him a place where he could lay down. "I just need a minute to catch my breath," he said. Well, one of the problems with having a bodyguard is he gets to know you too well, and he gets too sensitive about all the little signs and symptoms. I slipped out of his hearing range and made a call to our dispatcher. He must have been on call, because Dr. Nelson was there in what seemed like minutes. He spent some time checking the President out. In time, he told me I could take the President home. As soon as we were alone in the car, he began to dress me down. He was, at least for him, being pretty stern.

He clearly wanted to impress on me how unhappy he was. He said I was never to do something like that again. "President," I said. "Don't even try to put me into that position. My responsibility is not just to protect you from dangerous people. I am also responsible for your health and well-being. Whenever you appear to be in need of medical care, I will be calling for medical help. I will be obedient to you in every way. You tell me to shoot myself in the foot, I'll do it! But keeping you alive is my number one priority—it is even ahead of keeping you happy." There was a long silence in the car—at least it seemed long to me. When he did start talking again, it was about something else entirely. He never brought the subject up again.

There is another story that probably needs to be told, because it will be helpful to a select audience. One night, as we were changing security after my day had ended and the night man was taking charge, we found ourselves standing out in front of the residence sharing some security information. Much to our embarrassment, we noticed a man had slipped past us and was heading for the front door. We both rushed to cut him off before he could get there. We didn't make it, and he had already knocked on the door as we got there. President Kimball opened the door as I was in the process of explaining why he would not be allowed to stay and visit. "Please let him in," President Kimball said. "He is a friend, and he needs to see me." Well, of course I let him in. However, I stood on the stairs for the two hours the man stayed.

The next morning, as we drove to the office, I asked for some kind of an explanation. Understanding that it was a security issue, President Kimball gave me an explanation. Apparently, this man had been visiting the President off and on for a considerable number of years. He was a member of the Church, and he had a problem with homosexuality. It wasn't an everyday problem, but one that overcame him once in a while. Generally, he was able to keep the problem under control for weeks and months at a time. Then, on one less careful night he would lose control, and as soon as the moment passed, he would travel up to the President's residence. It seemed that only by talking with President Kimball could he find the strength to get him back on line. President Kimball never seemed to lose hope or patience. The notion of seventy times seventy was not just some notion to President Kimball. His love was truly for all mankind. He was willing to work with this man forever, if necessary.

Once a year, the Beneficial Life Insurance Company held their annual convention. The Church owned most of its stock, and President Kimball was their chairman. So, as he was to be the keynote speaker, we loaded up and headed for Colorado. While we were in Colorado, our host was Doug Smith. I believe he was the President of Beneficial Life at that time. President and Sister Kimball spent most of the time with Doug and Barbara Smith. Even though I was generally seen as something of a shadow, Doug and Barbara treated me more like family. I got so comfortable around them that I found myself referring to them as friends in my journal. To say they were wonderful people doesn't even begin to them into proper focus.

Being a bodyguard is, for the most part, a very uncomfortable place to be. No one ever quite seems to know how to treat you or what to do with you. Every place the prophet goes, he will be asked to sit up front. The six foot rule kicks in, and people will be asked to shuffle the seating arrangements so that the bodyguard (who, like the army's Delta Force, doesn't officially exist) can be seated next to the President. Even something as simple as eating out at a restaurant always requires some reshuffling. I became used to being treated as a robot or some other kind of problem.

Being around the Smiths was a totally new and wonderful experience. Nothing ever had to be reshuffled because they had me worked into all of their planning. I remember the first night in Colorado. We spent the whole evening with the Smiths in their room playing a child's game called "Rook." Of course I didn't play because I was on duty. Still, it was great just watching them laugh and play jokes on one another. Even though it was all about having fun, President showed another side of himself. He played to win. He was, while at all times laughing, playing, and having fun, still aggressive in his style and approach. We were all up late that night, and it showed the next day. President Kimball was pretty much the first real speaker, and he had to be careful not to let anyone see his fatigue.

A little before it was time for him to go on, we ran into a small snag. The Beneficial Life officials had purchased a number of sports jackets that were handed out to top sales people and the visiting speakers. The jacket was royal blue and made of polyester. It had rather broad stitching of another lighter blue surrounding the outer edges of the jacket. My guess is they toned it down just for President Kimball, but apparently not enough. It took D. Arthur twenty minutes to talk the President into putting it on—he was a very conservative man. He always reminded me, "The suit is the uniform of the priesthood." Because he held that attitude, he was very particular about how he should look when representing the priesthood. He favored conservative colors such as black, blue, and gray. Even pinstripe would do, so long as it was not too broad. The suit should be in the background; it should never announce itself. He finally gave in and wore the Beneficial jacket, though, because he worried about offending others even more. I very much doubt that he ever wore it again.

One day, as we were leaving the office, the President leaned over to me and said, "Let's make a stop over at the Smith's." Then, to be sure I knew who he meant, he added, "Doug and Barbara's." I drove to the Smiths, got out, and helped him inside. We were on a security high alert that day, so I returned to the car where I could cover the situation better. In a short while, Doug came out and began to visit with me. I didn't think too much about it because that was just the kind of guy he was. Later, the President came out, and we resumed our travel home. He leaned over and shared with me that she had agreed to be the next general Relief Society President. I couldn't have been happier if she had been my own mother. To this day, I still think of the Smith's as my friends.

# 11

---

# Travel Abroad

"Is there not wisdom in his giving us trials that we might rise above them, responsibilities that we might achieve . . . that we might be immortalized and glorified?"

—Spencer W. Kimball[1]

In Chapter Five, it was easy to talk about my assignment in terms of daily routine, but when President Kimball traveled abroad, the word "routine" became much harder to pin down or define. Clearly, there was a schedule or itinerary, but things had a way of changing—sometimes from minute to minute. I had to stay much more flexible. It would be very confusing to try to tell about several different trips abroad, so I chose one—our biggest trip—that should be representative of the rest.

In 1975, it was decided that the concept of an Area Conference abroad might be expanded into several Area Conferences, but all on the same continent—in this case, South America. We all boarded commercial airlines from Salt Lake City to the first major stop in Venezuela. We made our landing at the airport, which was pretty much at sea level. I stepped off the plane expecting to see the city of Caracas right in front of me. To my surprise, we loaded up in vehicles to begin an ascent up the mountain. As it turns out, Caracas is way up the mountain above the airport.

We settled into our hotel rooms and prepared for a special meal that was to be given in honor of President Kimball. During that first social situation in South America, I was introduced as President Kimball's bodyguard. This was very surprising to me as I was used to being "undercover." As it turned out, there was little effort to explain away my presence the whole time we were in South America. No one ever explained that different approach to me. I have since wondered if it wasn't because all leaders, at least the leaders of foreign governments, had scores of bodyguards. Maybe, to be thought of as important, President Kimball needed to have at the very least a couple of bodyguards.

Not too long before this trip got underway, the director of security for the Church retired. It seemed a great loss. He had been very dependable and helpful to us in our efforts to design and implement security for the President. About a week or two later, a new director, Earl Jones, was put in his place. Earl had been the Chief of Police of Salt Lake City. He had gotten crosswise with another member of the City Council and had been replaced by a new Chief. The Brethren jumped at the opportunity to ask him to step into the security directorship for the Church.

Anyway, the budget for this trip would only handle a limited number of security guards. One of the first things Earl did as the new director was reorganize the President's security abroad around himself. D. Arthur made it abundantly clear that I would be going as the six-foot perimeter man, but Earl would be the only other member of security who would be traveling on this trip. Since it was made clear that I would be the one next to the President, Earl assigned himself the job of traveling ahead to arrange the security coverage in the next country we would be visiting. When we arrived in Caracas, Earl had already been there and had set up security for the time we would be in Venezuela.

The local security was made up of members who were either in law enforcement or the military. These men took their responsibility very seriously, as it would likely be the one time in their lives where they would be able to serve their own Prophet. The main downside to this approach was that by the time these faithful members got over the thrill and excitement of being around the Prophet and began to provide quality security coverage, we were moving on to the next stop and the process would begin all over again.

The next day, we found ourselves flying over the jungles of northern Brazil. Sister Kimball, who knew a little about my background teaching jungle survival in Panama, said, "Well, at least if this plane goes down here in the jungles, we have Larry to keep us alive." I'm not sure the President knew what she was talking about. While she and I had talked about it, I don't remember if I ever shared that part of my past with him.

It was a long way across the Amazon Basin and the Brazilian Highlands before we finally landed in Rio de Janeiro. We had more meetings with members, leaders, missionaries, and mission presidencies. The President loved the people so much, it seemed he could never get enough of them. My assignment as his security, however, got much harder, because Latin males are traditionally much more demonstrative in showing their love toward their leaders. I had become used to members coming forward with an outstretched arm, hoping to shake hands as a show of affection. In South America, they come forward with both hands outstretched, expecting great shows of hugging or as it is known in the area as *embrasso*.

Well, let me just say that as a bodyguard, it is a lot harder to protect against physical attack when throngs of people are crowding the man you are trying to protect. Not only was there a fear from an intentional attack, but many of these men doing the hugging were going at it with little or no physical restraint; they were, at times, crushing the life out of him. I began to see my role switch from that of a smiling-but-cautious observer to that of a highly charged, defensive tackle. Many times, I had to insert myself between an overly aggressive member and my President. To my surprise, he never criticized me or even gave me a little "it's okay" look as he so often did when I got too protective. The message to me was, "Thanks, Larry. Please help me out whenever you can." I did!

While the main party came together in Rio, the President made a brief trip to the Capitol, Brasilia, to visit with the leading government administrators, where he was able to iron out some missionary issues. Before leaving Rio, he and Sister Kimball were able to do a little sightseeing. By nature, training, and responsibility, I am a keen observer; whenever we were touring, I was careful not to miss anything. However, on this particular trip, I remember looking pretty much straight ahead. We drove the full length of Ipapnema Beach with our driver pointing out all the features. I sat on the passenger side, up front, next to the window. The beach was at my right, and so were the bathing suits—or the lack thereof. With the Prophet of the Lord right behind me, it seemed clear to me that the right thing to do in this situation was to look straight ahead. I think that may have been one of the most uncomfortable rides I have ever had in my life. I might be wrong, but I'm guessing that my President was chuckling under his breath, fully aware of my discomfort. Not a word was ever spoken about it.

The next stop on our itinerary was Asunción, Paraguay. I remember the hotel there better than any other on the whole trip because it was a bit like stepping back into the old American western frontier. There was even a water pitcher and bowl in my room for cleaning up.

One of the first meetings attended was for missionaries. President Kimball was the chief speaker, but for some reason I've never had adequately explained to me, there was a spot in the program where someone didn't show. President Kimball asked me to get up and fill that spot. I argued with him that I could not provide security coverage for him standing at the pulpit. I never won an argument with him before, and things were no different on that occasion. I can't remember even today what subject I spoke on, but I do remember that a few people were kind enough to thank me after. That night, I put together a talk I could carry with me, so I would be prepared the next time he took it into his mind to get me on my feet. As scary as that might seem, it paled in significance next to the time, a few days later, where President Kimball decided to ask me to step up. We were always called into the President's bedroom at bedtime for family prayer. On this particular night, the people in the room were President and Sister Kimball, President and Sister Tanner, three Apostles and their wives, several other General Authorities and their wives, D. Arthur Haycock and Sister Haycock, and last and really least, me. When President Kimball said, "Larry would you mind saying the prayer?" I nearly passed out. Now, why should that have been so terrifying? I never really figured it out, but trust me, it was!

I can promise you in all the time I was in President Kimball's presence—which was most of his daylight hours—I never saw him angry, and I never heard him chew anyone out. He did, however, have a soft and subtle way to get his displeasure across. An example of that happened in Asunción. We had all taken our seats to eat breakfast or lunch, but before we got any further, the mission president, President Marchant (I think), started to talk to President Kimball, so he stood to be closer. He was safe, standing right next to me, so I dropped my head (as I had learned to do from President Kimball over the last year), said a silent prayer, and began to eat. The General Authority seated next to me snapped, "We don't eat around here until the prayer has been said." Before I could do or say anything, President Kimball sat down next to me, dropped his head, said a silent prayer, and began to eat. His actions caught those around me somewhat by surprise. However, nothing else was said as others silently prayed and began to eat. That was my President and one of the reasons I loved him so much.

While we were in Paraguay, we had an invitation to meet with the president of Paraguay, a man named Stroessner (as I recall). Our small party entered a waiting room outside his office. Seated all around the room were men brandishing lots and lots of serious firearms. Most were wearing handguns in shoulder holsters, some single, many double. Assault rifles and machine guns stood next to each chair. These guys made Mafia hit men look like grade school children. President Kimball and D. Arthur went in to meet with President Stroessner and left me to spend the next hour in a stare down with twenty or so men who probably thought they could eat me for breakfast. Still, I reasoned that some of the image President Kimball would leave with the leaders of this country would include whatever level of security he could afford. So, I did my best to convey a sense of confidence. Later in the day, one of the hotel employees (who, as it turned out, was a nephew of one of President Stroessner's security guards) told me the men in that room had wondered out loud if I was some kind of James Bond. I guess my acting was better than I had hoped.

The next place on our itinerary (as I recall) was back to Brazil, but this time to San Paulo, where the first official Area Conference was to be held. We left the airport in Paraguay in a plane that looked a little suspect even on the runway. Not too long after we got up to altitude, we began experiencing problems with an engine. While the ground beneath us it wasn't exactly jungle, but it was not a place we wanted to explore firsthand. The pilot turned the plane back with lavish apologies. President Kimball made some remark about it being better to turn back then to end up in the jungle. Our second try was a success. The one thing that sticks in my mind about that trip was how long it took to fly over San Paulo. I remember looking down at a large settled city. The pilot announced that we were over San Paulo—we then continued to fly over and over the city headed I'm sure in one direction for what seemed like hours. If San Paulo is not the largest city in the world, it's certainly the most spread out.

Well, up to that point in time, we had spent our time in visits to members, leaders, and missionaries, but now it was time to do what we had come for—our Area Conference. We were going to be holding it in a large soccer area. Because we were planning to be San Paulo for more than just a day or two, Earl stayed and became a real part of the on-site security team. As usual, he had arranged for a lot of local security. This was a great help because wherever we went we were surrounded with security. Although this will sound strange to the average member, it was really the members who posed more of a threat to the President than did the extremists. The danger was not of intentional harm but of being so intense about their desire to get close to their prophet that they became part of a crushing force that could harm just as surely as a bullet. Having this large contingent of security around him at all times reduced that problem. It also helped that they were mostly active law enforcement professionals who were not afraid to throw a little muscle into the situation when it was called for.

Now, having set the stage in this manner, I will tell you how exceptions to careful planning occur. At the close of the first day, we were ready to exercise a carefully laid out plan to exit the area without putting the President in danger. Remember, we had nearly twenty highly trained law enforcement personnel fully briefed and ready to carry out their part of the plan. As soon as the official hand shaking was over, we would move as a group into the hall behind the stand, and then move quickly to the right for about twenty feet. We would then move left into a long, narrow hall that opened into a secure area where cars were waiting for the President's party. We would then be off to the hotel without anyone even knowing where we had gone. Now, let's get to what actually happened.

As we stepped out into the hall, an unbriefed General Authority (his name will remain anonymous) stepped forward. Grasping President Kimball by the arm, the man swung him to the left and proceeded to virtually drag him down the hall into the large foyer—and I do mean large. My guess is that there was well over a thousand people in that foyer. Well, that little maneuver had accomplished several things. First, it had cut the President and his party off from all of his security except Earl and I. It had also cut him off from all of the other General Authorities in his group, meaning members of the First Presidency and members of the Twelve. In fact, there was only President and Sister Kimball, D. Arthur and Sister Haycock, Earl Jones, me, and, of course, the unnamed General Authority. As soon as we popped into the foyer, everyone began to surge forward, hoping to get closer. For those in the rear, they were hoping just to see him. Well, such a crowd creates thousands of pounds of pressure, all focused in the center. Those members in the front rows began to see what was happening and tried to push back against the crowd to their rear, but to no avail. About this time I thought to myself, "It's just me and Earl."

One sister lost her baby out of her arms, and the baby fell into the milling crowd. Earl, bless his quick-thinking heart, dove down under the crowd and managed to recover the frightened, but unharmed baby. Unfortunately, we had moved on inside the press, and Earl was no longer close enough to provide any support. Sister Kimball's eyes were bigger than I ever saw them being. She was clearly terrified. I began smashing my way through the crowd (not a good way for one member to act toward another). I could see the sunlight coming through the big exit doors, and I was focused on getting my party out of all this alive and well. No one even tried to make social contact because those close enough could clearly see the danger to all involved.

In time, we all made it to the door. A short distance away, there were several buses lined up waiting for General Authorities and other administrators not part of the President's original party. We made our way to the nearest bus and got everyone on board. The President and I were the last to get on the bus. While standing on the steps of the bus, President Kimball turned back to the unnamed General Authority still standing outside the bus and said "Elder, don't you ever do anything like that again." I think that was the most harsh and severe chewing out I ever heard come from him. As I recall, the elder chose to get back to his lodging some other way.

For me, one of the real highlights of our visit to San Paulo was the day we drove out to dedicate the temple site for the first temple to be built in South America. It was a beautiful site and most of the member present shed tears of joy. It was a wonderful day for all of us. It made the Area Conference in Brazil just a little extra special. But it was over too soon and we were preparing to move on to the next conference. Since there were only a couple of actual Area Conferences, we visited almost every country in South America.

From San Paulo we flew to Montevideo, Uruguay and had many important meetings there. Earl had been there and had setup the security for us. Then he moved on to Buenos Aires, Argentina for the next Area Conference. When we arrived in Buenos Aires, a full compliment of security was in place and already at work. I was very grateful for Earl's efforts and successes and most grateful for all the high quality help, but for the first time I experienced a strange feeling of regret. At first, I couldn't put my finger on the reason for my negative response, but then it started to become clear. I was becoming less indispensable, less vital to this effort.

During the Area Conference in Argentina, the President had announced the construction of a new temple in San Paulo, and the Saints in Argentina were very upset. They countered that a General Authority had, many years before, promised that the first temple would be built in Buenos Aires. It seemed, however, no one could find proof of that promise, other than hearsay. President Kimball was a little stern, at least for him. He told them that they did not have the numbers to justify a temple and that they should go to work and be better missionaries. They needed more stakes, more wards, and most of all, more members. "Temples are built," he said, "when, and only when, the membership justifies the expenditure."

One of the strange things, as far as my responsibility was concerned, was that Argentina was the place where the most serious threats to President Kimball occurred. President Tanner was scheduled to travel up to Mendoza to meet with the members. Our local security guys were top administrators in local and national law enforcement. They got word than an effort would be made to kidnap President Tanner, so we had to divide our forces—one would go to Mendoza and one would stay behind. Even back in Buenos Aires, things were spooky. There were threats every day. Explosives were found, and other attempts were discovered. On one hand, it was nice having the top cops in the country on your own security team, but the downside, if indeed there was a downside, was too much intelligence information. Anyway, it kept me hopping the whole time we were in Argentina. One good thing was that we had learned a good lesson from the unnamed General Authority in San Paulo. We kept a very large circle of huge, strong, highly trained men all around the President everywhere we went. If there was going to be any danger, it would come from extremists, not well-intentioned members. The things I remember best about Argentina were some of the great friends I made with some of our "top cops," and, of course, really good beef steaks. When it comes to great beef, Kansas City's got nothing on Buenos Aires.

Finally, the time came to pick up and move. Most of the Brethren would be going home. While there was a heavy contingent of General Authorities for the Area Conferences, the many stops to other countries consisted pretty much of just the President and his party. We flew to Santiago, Chile, for some meetings with the members. From Chile, we flew over several countries, mostly for security reasons. We flew over Peru and Ecuador, and landed in Bogota, Columbia, where a great many members crowded the airport terminal with banners to meet and greet the President. The mission president was Elder Franklin D. Richardson's son. We stayed in the mission home and spent more time in meetings with the members and leaders.

The altitude in Bogota is very high and President Kimball required an oxygen tank, especially at night, to provide additional oxygen so he could sleep. During the day, he got to spend time with some of the indigenous Indians who were members of the Church. He enjoyed that time very much and, for once, they were all shorter than him. I think he was always a little sensitive about his height because the Kimballs generally tended to be taller generally.

Well, Colombia was the last stop on the big South American trip of 1975. We returned home, and as soon as I got President and Sister Kimball safe at home, I turned their security over to the night man and made my way home to my family, who I had missed and was very anxious to be with. As an affirmation to my earlier premonition, my time with President Kimball had indeed come to an end.

1. Kimball, *Teachings of Spencer W. Kimball*, 39.

# About the Author

Lawrence Mullins grew up with his maternal grandparents. They were ranchers, so he grew up a ranch boy, developing the skills and abilities that come with growing up on a ranch. He graduated from Brigham Young University.

After his faithful service as the bodyguard to President Spencer W. Kimball, Larry spent nearly twenty-four years as ranger for the state of Utah. During that time he also served as a reserve deputy for the Daggett County Sheriff's office. He was an instructor for many POST classes, served as the range commander on many handgun, shotgun, and sniper training courses, and served as the county underwater dive commander, the county tracker, and, in addition, served several years as the EMT trainer and coordinator.

Larry has served as an elders quorum president, a seventy, a gospel doctrine teacher, high priest group leader, stake high councilor, stake presidency counselor, CES instructor, a counselor in a student ward bishopric, and temple ordinance worker.

0  26575 53368  2